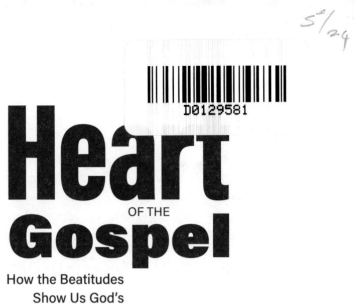

D0129581

Heart
OF THE
Gospel

How the Beatitudes
Show Us God's
Plan for Happiness

By Sebastian Walshe, O. Praem.

Catholic
Answers
Press

Published by Catholic Answers, Inc.
2020 Gillespie Way
El Cajon, California 92020
1-888-291-8000 orders
619-387-0042 fax
catholic.com

Printed in the United States of America

Cover design by Theodore Schluenderfritz
Interior design by Russell Graphic Design

978-1-68357-310-4
978-1-68357-311-1 Kindle
978-1-68357-312-8 ePub

To Mary, cause of our joy

CONTENTS

THE WAY TO HAPPINESS

If you're like me, the first time you ever took the trouble to learn the Beatitudes it was a list you had to memorize in catechism class. For most people, that is all the Beatitudes has been: a list, and now likely a forgotten list.

My hope is that this book will change all of that. My hope is that as you read this book you will see how the Beatitudes were at the very heart of the teaching of Jesus Christ, and that they are a not a memorization exercise but a way of life to be lived.

The world first heard the Beatitudes proclaimed overlooking the Sea of Galilee, in the Sermon on the Mount, and they are as central to the teaching of Jesus as the Ten Commandments, given on Mount Sinai, were to the teaching of Moses. Everything Jesus taught originates from and returns to the Beatitudes. In short, the Beatitudes are the Gospel, the good tidings, which Jesus came to preach, and all of his moral teachings are fulfilled in them. Becoming and being a Christian is simply the living-out of the Beatitudes more and more fully. Yet they will only be *perfectly* lived in the life to come.

Happiness: the ultimate reason for living

Beatitude is a fancy name for happiness. It comes from the Latin word *beatitude,* a kind of happiness that is more than emotional satisfaction; it includes the sense of *blessedness.* In the scriptures, the Greek word Jesus uses at the beginning of each Beatitude is *makarioi,* which implies a kind of all-inclusive happiness that satisfies the deepest longings of the human heart and even transcends the possibilities of human nature. In fact, the same word is used in the New Testament to describe God's happiness as well as the heavenly happiness of Jesus (see, for example, 1 Timothy 1:11 and 6:15). So when Jesus tells us in the Beatitudes that we are or will be *blessed*, he is telling us about a transcendent happiness that is a share in the very happiness of Jesus Christ and the Most Holy Trinity.

This kind of happiness is the meaning of life, and the ultimate goal of our every desire and choice. Sometimes we can lose sight of this fundamental fact. Our search for happiness is like the air we breathe: we are unconsciously looking for it in every decision we make, yet we can get so preoccupied with the particular things we think will get us to happiness that we sometimes fail to appreciate that ultimately it's not this or that *thing* that we really want, but rather happiness itself. And if we understood that the particular good we are striving after won't actually make us happy, we would stop seeking it right away.

When I teach ethics to high school students, I try to teach them this lesson by asking a series of questions. Usually, the dialogue goes something like this:

Teacher: Why are you sitting in my class right now?

Student: Because I want to get a good grade.

Teacher: Why do you want good grades?

Student: Because I want to get into a good college.

Teacher: And why do you want to get into a good college?

Student: To get a good job.

Teacher: And why do you want to get a good job?

Student: To make lots of money.

Teacher: And why do you want to make lots of money?

Student: [*Feeling a bit of frustration and saying to himself, "Isn't it obvious why I want to make a bunch of money?! Everyone wants a bunch of money!"*] Why do I want lots of money?! Because it gives me the freedom to do whatever I want!

Teacher: And why do you want to be able to do whatever you want?

Student: Because I want to be happy!

Teacher: Finally, we have reached the ultimate reason: happiness. Everything you do, you do because you want to be happy. And if you found out that making lots of money would not make you happy, but rather *un*happy, would you still choose to make a lot of money?

Student: I guess not . . . but it *will* make me happy!

Teacher: That remains to be seen. To know whether that is true or not, you have to know what happiness *is*. So can you tell me: What is happiness?

Student: Ummm . . . [crickets] . . .

In the Beatitudes, Jesus gives us the answer to that question. He is someone uniquely qualified to answer it because, as God, he made us, so he knows what will fulfill us; and as man, he experienced the most perfect happiness possible, so we can follow him to the same destination.

The necessity of following Jesus is even more manifest when we come to realize that the working of the human heart is counterintuitive. We expect it to work one way, when in fact it works the opposite way. The Lord expressed this well when he spoke through the prophet Jeremiah: "More tortuous than all else is the human heart, beyond remedy; who can understand it? I, the Lord, alone probe the mind and test the heart" (Jer. 17:9–10, NAB).

Some years ago, I read an article about a remarkable item: the Antikithera device, discovered more than a hundred years ago in the waters off the shore of Greece. In the remains of a shipwreck that was dated to the first century B.C., explorers found a complex machine about the size of a shoebox. But because the machine was so covered with rust and grime, and because it was so complex, scientists were at a complete loss about its function. Only many years later, with the advent of specialized x-ray technology, were scientists able to discover an entire system of gears and levers within the box and thus reconstruct it from scratch. To their astonishment, they discovered that the machine was an astronomical clock that could accurately predict the motions and positions of the heavenly bodies for centuries in advance, including solar and lunar eclipses. Nothing of comparable sophistication would be found in the Western world until the fourteenth century! It certainly would have been easier for those scientists if they had found an instruction manual for that machine. But as it was, it took almost a century to figure out how it worked.

Something similar happened to the human heart. At the dawn of our race, there was a great shipwreck, and among the things that went down with the ship was the human heart. So damaged was the human heart by the wound of original sin that its full potential for happiness and love remained largely unknown until Jesus came with the instruction manual for the human heart: the Beatitudes. While men were vainly seeking happiness in wealth, Jesus came with the instruction *blessed are the poor in spirit*. While men were vainly seeking happiness in the fleeting pleasures of the emotions, Jesus came with the instruction *blessed are those who mourn*. While men were vainly seeking happiness in the esteem of men, Jesus came with the instruction *blessed are you when men reproach you and persecute you.*

Truly, the human heart is counterintuitive, and without Jesus we could not have found happiness on our own. We were like flies vainly seeking the light of the sun through a windowpane when the way out was an open door through the darkness right behind us.

1

THE BEATITUDES IN SCRIPTURE

Scripture is God's word. This means it is an expression of the mind of God in human language. The great analogy for Scripture is the incarnate Word of God himself, Jesus Christ. Just as the Word of God became like man in all things but sin, so the word of God becomes like human language in all things but error. So Sacred Scripture is language that is fully human and fully divine, just as Jesus is fully man and fully God.[1] With this in mind, it is important to read Scripture reverently and with attention to the context as well as all the details. Jesus is speaking to us whenever we read Scripture. Among other things, this means that all of the details have meaning, including the setting and context of the text.

The setting

In Matthew's Gospel, the primary source for the Beatitudes, we find Jesus teaching, healing, and casting out demons such that people were coming to him from all over:

"Great crowds followed him from Galilee and the Decapolis and Jerusalem and Judea and from beyond the Jordan" (Matt. 4:25). The places listed more or less correspond to the boundaries of the Promised Land parceled out by Moses to the twelve tribes of Israel (Num. 34). So the implication is that representatives from the whole of God's people were following Jesus at this time.

When he saw the crowd, Jesus "went up on the mountain, and when he sat down his disciples came to him" (Matt. 5:1). Here, Matthew quotes Exodus 19:3, where Moses goes up Mount Sinai (see also Exodus 24:18 and 34:4). Another interesting detail is that Matthew uses the definite article, calling it *the* mountain. Normally, the definite article is used for two reasons: either because it is referring to some preceding thing (for example, some preceding mention of a mountain) or because the thing modified by the definite article is the instance of that thing *par excellence* (as if we were to say of some man "he is *the* man"). But there is no preceding mention of a mountain in this text, suggesting that Matthew is speaking about this mountain as *the* mountain before all others.

All of these things call to mind the event on Mount Sinai when God delivered the Law to Moses, who in turn communicated it to the people. So Matthew wants to tell us that the Sermon on the Mount is the delivering of the New Law, and just as the Ten Commandments were at the heart of the Old Law, so now the eight Beatitudes are at the heart of the New. These details underline how central the Beatitudes are to the teaching of Christ. Pope St. Leo the Great agrees:

> He separated himself from the surrounding crowds, ascended into the retirement of a neighboring mountain, and called his apostles to him there, that from the height of that

mystic seat he might instruct them in the loftier doctrines, signifying from the very nature of that place and act that he it was who had once honored Moses by speaking to him. Then, indeed, with a more terrifying justice, but now with a holier mercifulness that what had been promised might be fulfilled when the prophet Jeremiah says: "Behold, the days come when I will complete a new covenant with the house of Israel and for the house of Judah. . . . After those days, says the Lord, I will put my laws in their minds, and in their heart I will write them" [Jer. 31:31, 33]. He, therefore, who had spoken to Moses spoke also to the apostles, and the swift hand of the Word wrote and deposited the secrets of the new covenant in the disciples' hearts.

The sermon

The Sermon on the Mount related in Matthew 5–7 has much in common with the teaching of Jesus related in Luke 6. It is widely recognized that Luke 6 teaches in an abbreviated form what Matthew 5–7 teaches in greater detail. But there are also some significant differences. The sermon of Luke 6 takes place on a plain, whereas the sermon of Matthew 5–7 takes place on a mountain. There are also differences between the Beatitudes themselves in the two accounts. Luke recounts only four Beatitudes and follows them with four corresponding woes, whereas Matthew recounts eight Beatitudes and offers no complementary woes (though he does pronounce some woes in chapter 23). Moreover, the four Beatitudes pronounced in Luke are all addressed immediately to the crowd, "Happy are you," whereas the eight Beatitudes pronounced in Matthew are announced in the third person, "Blessed are they" (with one notable exception that I will address later).

St. Augustine provides two possible explanations for these differences. One possibility is that although only one sermon was delivered, its location was described under different aspects by Matthew and Luke. For it is possible that the place was a level spot along the slope of the mountain, which at once was part of the mountain and might also be described as a plain in relation to the peak of the same mountain. According to this account, the sermon as related by Matthew included a number of our Lord's words that Luke omitted and omitted some of the words that Luke included.

A second solution is that Jesus actually gave two sermons that were closely related: for his purpose was to promulgate the New Law, yet not all were prepared to receive that law in its most perfect form. Therefore, since the first promulgation was given only to his close disciples on the mountaintop, it was lengthier and more proportioned to the spiritual-minded; and since the second was given to the multitudes on the plain, it was shorter and more proportioned to the carnal-minded.

In what follows, I will focus primarily upon the more complete account of the Beatitudes reported by Matthew, but I will also consider some of the elements recorded by Luke.

Matthew records the Beatitudes in these words:

Seeing the crowds, [Jesus] went up on the mountain, and when he sat down his disciples came to him. And he opened his mouth and taught them, saying:

Blessed are the poor in spirit, for theirs is the kingdom of heaven.

Blessed are those who mourn, for they shall be comforted.

Blessed are the meek, for they shall inherit the earth.[2]

Blessed are those who hunger and thirst for righteousness, for they shall be satisfied.

Blessed are the merciful, for they shall obtain mercy.

Blessed are the pure in heart, for they shall see God.

Blessed are the peacemakers, for they shall be called sons of God.

Blessed are those who are persecuted for righteousness' sake, for theirs is the kingdom of heaven. Blessed are you when men revile you and persecute you and utter all kinds of evil against you falsely on my account. Rejoice and be glad, for your reward is great in heaven, for so men persecuted the prophets who were before you (Matt. 5:1–12, ESV).

A few observations are in order before we dig into this text more deeply. Notice that the occasion of the teaching of these Beatitudes was Jesus seeing the crowds. It does not say that he sat down then and there and taught the crowds. Rather it says that he went up the mountain and then his disciples came to him. This seems to indicate that Jesus somehow separated himself from the crowds for a time and only his disciples came up to the mountain with him to hear this sermon, not the entire crowd. This implies two things. First, that this sermon is directed at those who were already his disciples; those who were already accustomed to hearing Jesus preach. This accounts for the detail and advanced spiritual doctrine contained in Matthew's account of the Sermon on the Mount. In contrast, Luke's account is abbreviated and not as spiritually advanced. All of this points to the likelihood that there were two sermons given: one on the mount to his disciples, and a second on the plain to the whole people.

The second thing this introduction implies is that Jesus is trying to impress upon his disciples how blessed this poor and indigent crowd really is. One can imagine that Jesus' disciples might have found many in the crowd to be repulsive or at least off-putting. After all, many of them were sick, and most were probably jobless and needy. The usual situation of these crowds is that they ended up with not enough food to eat. So Jesus is teaching his disciples to look upon them with his eyes, to see them as they truly are: blessed by God.

Looking at the Beatitudes themselves, a number of initial questions come to mind. What is a Beatitude? How many Beatitudes are there? Are there other Beatitudes found in Scripture? Is Jesus talking about happiness in this life or the next? Are these Beatitudes talking about what happiness is or what it is not? Is it enough to keep one Beatitude, or do we have to abide by all of them to become happy? Is there some determinate order to these eight Beatitudes? What does each Beatitude mean? Who are the people addressed in each of the eight Beatitudes? Why do so many of the Beatitudes speak about painful experiences such as poverty, sadness, hunger, and persecution, and how are these reconcilable with being perfectly happy?

I will attempt to answer each of these questions, as well as others, in what follows. The general questions I will attempt to answer in the remainder of this chapter, and the questions pertaining to each Beatitude in particular I will attempt to answer in the chapter dedicated to that Beatitude.

What is a Beatitude?

A Beatitude is a brief instruction from our Lord in Scripture, given in poetic form, that teaches us how to find lasting and divine happiness. Moreover, since the happiness described in these Beatitudes is the ultimate goal of human life, and since nothing more than these Beatitudes seems to be necessary, we can conclude that the Beatitudes contain, in seminal form, the entire doctrine of Jesus Christ. Each Beatitude is composed of two parts: a *condition* that indicates the reason for merit and a *reward* that brings or causes happiness. Because God is just, every good deed has as its effect some appropriate reward. As King David proclaimed, "The Lord rewards every man for his righteousness and his faithfulness" (1 Sam. 26:23, ESV).[3]

Of course, the fact that merit is the condition for reward implies that evil actions are the condition for punishment. Therefore, in another place St. Paul writes, "We must all appear before the judgment seat of Christ, so that each one may receive good or evil, according to what he has done in the body" (2 Cor. 5:10). Consequently, for each Beatitude, there is a corresponding "woe." Luke expressly records the woes contrary to the Beatitudes, though Matthew does not.[4] This is probably because Matthew's Beatitudes were addressed to Jesus' disciples, who were already well disposed to following him; and so those who already followed Jesus out of love did not need fear to dissuade them from seeking the vanities of the world. But since the Beatitudes in Luke were addressed to the whole crowd, Jesus teaches them that they cannot sit upon the fence: either they practice the Beatitudes and find eternal joy, or they don't and find eternal misery. Following Jesus is an all-or-nothing proposition.

A friend of mine once observed that it is interesting that Christ thought it worthwhile to give his teaching in short form, in memorable sayings, and with the poetic elements of symmetry and repetition, like proverbs or even a song. This implies that he wants these things in our memory. He wants his words to stick. What remains in the memory continues to be a principle of our actions. The Beatitudes thus should constantly be in our minds and hearts.

How many Beatitudes are there?

Luke records four Beatitudes; Matthew records eight or nine. If Augustine (along with St. Thomas) is right, the discrepancy between Luke and Matthew can be accounted for by the fact that there were two different sermons. So on this account, Matthew's list is more complete, since it was proposed to the spiritually mature and therefore excludes all of the mistaken views of blessedness, even those that are more spiritual in nature. On the other hand, Luke only lists those Beatitudes necessary to exclude a more base view of blessedness, such as the view that it consists in wealth, or bodily pleasures, or some such thing. Thomas Aquinas explains it this way:

> Luke narrates that the sermon of the Lord was made to the crowds. Hence, the Beatitudes enumerated by him were those proposed to the capacity of the crowds, who knew only physically pleasant and temporal and earthly beatitude. Hence, the Lord excludes through these four Beatitudes those things that seem to pertain to the aforesaid kind of beatitude.[5]

Thus the lengthier account given by Matthew seems to be more complete.

There may be another reason why Luke records only four of the Beatitudes recounted by Matthew: Luke is specifically considering the priesthood of Christ and the worship due to God. Therefore, he relates the promulgation of the New Law especially as it pertained to the new priesthood and to worship. Because a priest is a mediator between men and God, he must in some way touch both extremes. Therefore, two perfections pertain especially to religious worship and the priesthood: purity of heart, whereby man is joined to God, and mercy, whereby man bends toward one's neighbor. St. James's epistle teaches this in 1:27, where he says, "Religion that is pure and undefiled before God and the Father, is this: to visit orphans and widows in their affliction" (this pertains to mercy) "and to keep oneself unstained from the world" (this pertains to purity of heart). Therefore, the first three Beatitudes listed by Luke pertain to the perfection of purity of heart, whereas the last pertains to the perfection of mercy.

According to either explanation, we can conclude that the more complete account of our Lord's teaching includes all of the Beatitudes enumerated by Matthew. But did Matthew list eight or nine Beatitudes? The last Beatitude reads:

> Blessed are those who are persecuted for righteousness' sake, for theirs is the kingdom of heaven. Blessed are you when men revile you and persecute you and utter all kinds of evil against you falsely on my account. Rejoice and be glad, for your reward is great in heaven, for so men persecuted the prophets who were before you (Matt. 5:10–12, ESV).

In this text, Jesus says the word *blessed* twice, as if there are two Beatitudes. But notice, the second time he speaks about blessedness, he does not do so in the same form as in the other Beatitudes, with a brief coupling of some condition for merit followed by a reward. Moreover, what he says seems to be an unpacking or explication of what he had already said about those who are persecuted for the sake of righteousness. Therefore, it seems that what we have here is not a new Beatitude but an explanation of the final

Beatitude. Notice also that in this one case, Jesus addresses his disciples directly, in the second person: "Blessed are *you*." This serves to impress the reality of this final Beatitude upon the hearts of his disciples, who would one day suffer all that Jesus says here. So this conclusion of the last Beatitude seems to be almost prophetic. And he uses the term *blessed* again as if to indicate that one who lives according to this final Beatitude is twice-blessed.

Granting that the list found in Matthew's Gospel comprises eight Beatitudes, is he describing eight kinds of blessedness or only one? Certainly, the rewards described seem to differ in some respect: the kingdom of heaven, the earth, comfort, satisfaction, mercy, etc., sound like different rewards. Yet, Scripture clearly teaches that God alone is the source of perfect happiness: "My soul, be at rest in God alone" (Ps. 62:6, NAB). So are there many rewards or only one? The answer is that the one reward that fulfills all our desires can be described under many aspects, since no single word or concept can describe it.[6] Just as something too large for our eyes to take in would have to be seen and described part-by-part to give some idea of the whole, so also the goodness of God must be described in partial ways, as the reward in each Beatitude, in order to give a better idea of the whole goodness of God.[7]

Thus, the "kingdom of heaven" signifies God's goodness as bestowed upon all the elect reigning in heaven. The "earth" signifies our resurrected bodies that shall be completely in harmony with God's will. The reward of "comfort" signifies God's goodness as satisfying our emotions and desires. The reward of "mercy" signifies that we shall experience God's goodness as the cause of the removal of every misery and evil to which we were once subject, especially sin. And each reward can be understood in a similar manner.

Are there other Beatitudes found in Scripture?

There is one final question about the number of Beatitudes. Many other places in Scripture record sayings promising blessedness on some condition. For example, we read in the book of Revelation: "Blessed is he who reads aloud the words of the prophecy, and blessed are those who hear, and who keep what is written therein" (1:3). Is this another Beatitude for those who hear, read, and observe what is written in the book of Revelation?

In fact, some form of the Greek word for *blessed* appears more than fifty times in the New Testament and more than fifty times in the Septuagint (Greek) text of the Old Testament. Yet in each case, the blessedness proclaimed can be reduced back to one of the eight Beatitudes proclaimed by the Lord in Matthew's Gospel. For all merit and every fitting reward pertains to the love of God. And someone can love God through active good works (the active life) or through contemplative prayer and union with God (the contemplative life). Therefore, since the Beatitudes recorded by Matthew encompass the whole of the active and contemplative life, every blessedness proclaimed elsewhere in Scripture is found somehow in these eight Beatitudes. St. Thomas explains it this way:

> It is necessary that all of the Beatitudes pronounced elsewhere in Scripture be reduced to these [eight] either with regard to the merit or with regard to the reward. For it is necessary that all of them pertain in some way either to the active or to the contemplative life. Therefore, when it is said, "Blessed is the man who is corrected by the Lord" (Job 5:17), this pertains to the Beatitude "Blessed are those who mourn." But when it is said, "Blessed is the man who does not follow the counsel of the impious"

(Ps. 1:1) this pertains to purity of heart. But where it is said, "Blessed is the man who finds wisdom," (Prov. 3:13) this pertains to the reward of the seventh Beatitude. And the same is clear about all of the other [Beatitudes] which one might bring forth.[8]

What Augustine once said about prayer and the Our Father could also be applied to the Beatitudes: "If you study every word of the petitions of Scripture, you will find, I think, nothing that is not contained and included in the Lord's Prayer. When we pray, then, we may use different words to say the same things, but we may not say different things."[9] Similarly, there may be Beatitudes expressed in different words in Scripture, but they promise the same things.

2

THE KIND OF HAPPINESS PROMISED

Now that we have a better idea of what a Beatitude is, and how many are found in Scripture, it is natural to ask next about what kind of happiness Jesus is talking about and promising in the Beatitudes.

Is Jesus talking about happiness in this life or the next?

Most of the Beatitudes refer to a future reward; for example, "Blessed are those who mourn, for they *shall be* comforted." But some of the Beatitudes seem to refer to a reward in the here and now: "Blessed are the poor in spirit, for theirs *is* the kingdom of heaven." This raises the natural question: Do the Beatitudes refer to the present or the future; and if they refer to the future, is it the next life or this life?

The very fact that Jesus uses both the present and future tense in the Beatitudes indicates that there is something both future and present in every Beatitude. This is consonant with the teachings of the New Testament as a whole, which instruct us that we should place our whole hope in the goods of the life to come and yet rejoice here and now in hope. St. John warns us in the strongest terms not to love the things of this world: "Do not love the world or the things in the world. If anyone loves the world, love for the Father is not in him" (1 John 2:15). One reason John gives for this is that the world is passing away. On the other hand, Scripture teaches us to place all our hope and desire in the goods of the life to come: "Set your hope fully upon the grace that is coming to you at the revelation of Jesus Christ" (1 Pet. 1:13). And yet, although our love and hope are set on things of the next life, we rejoice already in this life: "Without having seen him you love him; though you do not now see him you believe in him and rejoice with unutterable and exalted joy" (1 Pet. 1:8).

Hope brings the joy of the future into the present. A couple of simple examples illustrate this. Say you buy a lottery ticket, and as you sit down to watch the numbers come up, you find that you have all the right numbers! You have won $100 million! Now, the fact of the matter is that, right at that moment you don't have even one cent of that money, but because you have the ticket that will get you that money, you are already filled with joy. The certainty of your hope has turned future joy into present joy. Again, let's say that there is a young woman who is dating the man of her dreams. And one day, he kneels down, produces a ring, and proposes. The woman is filled with joy even though the actual marriage may be more than a year away. (In fact, women often report that the day of the proposal was more joyful than the actual day of the wedding!) So we see how *hope makes future joy present.*

The joy promised in the Beatitudes is like this: it is both future and present. It is future insofar as the goods we are promised are eternal goods of the life to come. It is present insofar as our hope for those goods is certain so that we already begin to experience in this life a foretaste of the goods to come. Yet the joy we ought to experience in this life through the Beatitudes should be much greater than any joy we could experience because we hope in some merely earthly good, like a winning lottery ticket or getting an engagement ring: for the good promised is worth so much more than any jackpot, and the one who promises is more worthy of trust than any fiancé!

Because the joy of the Beatitudes is both present and future, it is possible simultaneously to experience joy and sorrow: joy in our hope for the life to come and sorrow in the afflictions of this present life. This is what Paul teaches: "we ourselves, who have the first fruits of the Spirit, groan inwardly as we wait for adoption as sons, the redemption of our bodies. For in this hope we were saved" (Rom. 8:23–24).

St. Thomas summarizes aptly when he writes:

All the rewards [promised in the Beatitudes] will be perfectly consummated in the future life, but in the interim, even in this life they will begin in a certain manner. For the kingdom of heaven, as Augustine says, is able to be understood as the beginning of perfect wisdom, according as the Spirit begins to reign in them. The possession of the land signifies the good affection of a soul resting through its desire in the stability of a perpetual inheritance (signified by the "land"). They will be consoled in this life by sharing in the Holy Spirit who is called the Paraclete, that is, the Consoler. They will also be satisfied in this life by that food about which the Lord says: "My food is to do the will of my Father." In this life also, men will experience the mercy of God; and in this life, by means of purification of the mind's eye through the gift

26

of understanding, God is in a certain way able to be seen. Similarly, also in this life those who make peace by their own acts, thereby approaching to the likeness of God, are called "sons of God." Nevertheless, these will be more perfect in the heavenly fatherland.[10]

From this, we can glean a profound truth: the blessedness of this life is in a certain way *contiguous with the blessedness of the life to come.* There is not, as some would like to think, a complete discontinuity between this life and the next, so that one day we are immersed in the joys of this world and the next day immersed in the joys of heaven. Our growth in the spiritual life here below is meant to approach more and more a likeness of the life we will live in heaven. St. Faustina expresses this well in her diary where she writes:

> The great light that illumines the mind gives me a knowledge of the greatness of God; but it is not as if I were getting to know the individual attributes, as before—no, it is different now: in one moment, I come to know the entire essence of God. In that same moment, the soul drowns entirely in him and experiences a happiness as great as that of the chosen ones in heaven. Although the chosen ones in heaven see God face to face and are completely and absolutely happy, still their knowledge of God is not the same. God has given me to understand this. This deeper knowledge begins here on earth, depending on the grace [given], but to a great extent it also depends on our faithfulness to that grace. However, the soul receiving this unprecedented grace of union with God cannot say that it sees God face to face, because even here there is a very thin veil of faith, but so very thin that the soul can say that it sees God and talks with him. It is "divinized."[11]

Granted that in some way all of the Beatitudes refer to the next life and the present life, is there a special reason why two of the Beatitudes use the present tense when promising their reward? Yes. Both of these Beatitudes promise the *kingdom of heaven* (or in Luke's account, the kingdom of God). Jesus in his preaching spoke as if the kingdom of heaven were already beginning to be present here on earth: "The kingdom of heaven is at hand" (Matt. 10:7). Moreover, he says about the kingdom of God that it is already in our midst (Luke 17:21). Thus, those Beatitudes that have the kingdom of heaven as their reward are also present in a special way.

Jesus makes this very explicit in regard to the poor in spirit when he says, "There is no man who has left house or wife or brothers or parents or children, for the sake of the kingdom of God, who will not receive manifold more *in this time*, and in the age to come eternal life" (Luke 18:29–30; see Mark 10:30 and Matt. 19:29). In other words, Jesus will so abundantly supply the needs of those who have assumed the state of voluntary poverty that they will receive much more, even in *this life*, than they gave up. Those who are persecuted for the sake of Jesus also have a special reason why their joy is present. The reason is that there is an even greater certitude of future reward for those who voluntarily accept undergo persecution for the sake of Jesus. This is why St. Peter makes this Beatitude the measure of all joy: "Rejoice in so far as you share Christ's sufferings, that you may also rejoice and be glad when his glory is revealed. If you are reproached for the name of Christ, you are blessed, because the spirit of glory and of God rests upon you" (1 Pet. 4:13–14).

Are these Beatitudes talking about what happiness is or what it is not?

Most of the Beatitudes are counterintuitive. It is not intuitive that things like poverty, hunger, mourning, and persecution bring about happiness! In some way, the first half of each Beatitude seems to be making a claim about what Beatitude does *not* consist in. St. Thomas explains it this way:

> We find four opinions about Beatitude. Certain ones believe that it consists only in exterior things, such as in affluence of temporal things . . . Others believe that Beatitude consists in a man satisfying his will . . . Others say that perfect Beatitude consists in the virtues of the active life, while others say that it consists in the virtues of the contemplative life, namely of divine and understandable things, as Aristotle did. All of these opinions are false, although not in the same way. Therefore, the Lord rejects all of them.[12]

So each Beatitude is teaching us what happiness does not consist in. On the other hand, the reward promised does pertain to what happiness is: namely, some aspect of union with God, our ultimate good. So we can say that each Beatitude simultaneously teaches us what happiness is not and what it is.

Is it enough to keep one Beatitude, or do we have to abide by all of them to become happy?

A friend once quipped, "Ten commandments is a lot! Can I narrow it down to one or two?" Someone might ask the same question about the Beatitudes. Can we just try one or two of them? What if I am just pure of heart, or just a peacemaker? Can I keep my money and eat and drink and be merry?

The question is a fair one, since it seems that each Beatitude stands on its own. The pure of heart will see God, so what more is needed beyond purity of heart? On the other hand, Jesus expressly gives woes in Luke's Gospel for those who are rich, or who are filled, who are rejoicing in this world. So it would seem that failing in any one Beatitude would exclude us from happiness.

The fact is that, just as with the commandments and the virtues, to do any one of them well is to do them all, and to break any one of them involves rejecting all of them. James argues this way:

> Whoever keeps the whole law but fails in one point has become guilty of all of it. For he who said, "Do not commit adultery," said also, "Do not kill." If you do not commit adultery but do kill, you have become a transgressor of the law (James 2:10–11).

Something similar can be said about the virtues. St. Thomas compares the growth of the virtues to the growth of the fingers on a hand:

> All the virtues of one man are equal with a kind of equality of proportion, inasmuch as they grow equally in a man, just as the fingers of the hand are unequal according to quantity, but are equal according to proportion, since they grow proportionally.[13]

Both the commandments and the virtues form a unity: the commandments because of the one Lawgiver, the virtues because of the single virtue, charity, that moves them all. So too, the Beatitudes are united by the one goal that is their object, namely, God himself.

Some examples will help to illustrate this fact. Let's say someone is very generous to the poor, but at the same time he is committing adultery. Can he truly be said to be virtuous, at least with regard to the virtue of generosity? Since virtue requires not only an outward act but an inward motive and habit, the person who fails in the inward motive or habit cannot truly be called virtuous. The ultimate motive required for a virtuous act is love of God above all things, and someone who commits adultery does not love God above all things. Instead, he loves the pleasure from adultery more than God. Therefore, even when he gives to the poor, he is doing this from some other motive than the love of God. And so he does not truly possess the virtue of generosity.

Something similar can be said about the Beatitudes. If someone thinks he is pure of heart but is so attached to his wealth that he would rather forsake God than forsake his wealth, he is clearly deceived about his purity of heart. Therefore, it is not possible to experience one Beatitude while rejecting another, any more than it is possible to love and rejoice in some part of God without loving all of God. For God is one, and whatever aspect of God's goodness we love and rejoice in demands that we love and rejoice in every aspect of God's goodness. Whoever experiences one Beatitude experiences all of them, and whoever rejects one Beatitude rejects all of them.

Is there some reason for the order to these eight Beatitudes?

Since all of the Beatitudes are connected, so that you cannot fulfill one without fulfilling the others, it might seem that the order in which Jesus lists the Beatitudes does not matter. Maybe it doesn't matter which Beatitude we start with, since all lead to the same destination. On the other hand it seems unlikely that Jesus would simply haphazardly list eight Beatitudes without any particular reason for their order. After all, he is the very Wisdom of God, and wisdom "orders all things well" (Wis. 8:1). Pope St. Leo the Great saw these eight Beatitudes as progressive steps that ascend to greater holiness and happiness: "Whoever longs to attain to eternal blessedness can now recognize the steps that lead to that high happiness."[14]

If we examine the matter more carefully, it becomes obvious that there is a profound order among the Beatitudes. Recall that each Beatitude has some reason for merit as well as a promised reward. Here are the reasons for merit in the order Jesus gives them:

The poor in spirit

Those who mourn

The meek

Those who hunger and thirst for righteousness

The merciful

The pure in heart

The peacemakers

Those who are persecuted for the sake of righteousness

Those that come earlier seem to concern virtues governing our *own body* and *private goods*, those in the middle seem to concern virtues pertaining to the *common good* of our neighbor, and those at the end seem to concern virtues governing our *relationship to God*. For the poor in spirit do not seek happiness in wealth; those who mourn do not place their happiness in physical pleasures; and the meek do not seek happiness in satisfying the inclinations of anger.[15] These pertain to someone's private person. Those who hunger and thirst for justice seek to give what is due to their neighbor, and the merciful seek to go beyond even this to give what is more than just. These pertain to the common good of our neighbor. Finally, the pure of heart are single-heartedly fixed upon God as their end, whereas the peacemakers are those who so long for the life of divine contemplation that they even produce the condition necessary for a contemplative life for all, namely peace, without which it is impossible to contemplate divine things.

The last of the Beatitudes, those who are persecuted for the sake of righteousness, seems to indicate someone so fixed upon God that even persecution cannot separate them from the object of their love, as Paul says:

> What will separate us from the love of Christ? Will anguish, or distress, or persecution, or famine, or nakedness, or peril, or the sword? As it is written: "For your sake we are being slain all the day; we are looked upon as sheep to be slaughtered." No, in all these things we conquer overwhelmingly through him who loved us. For I am convinced that neither death, nor life, nor angels, nor principalities, nor present things, nor future things, nor powers, nor height, nor depth, nor any other creature will be able to separate us from the love of God in Christ Jesus our Lord (Rom. 8:35–39).

So we can see the way in which the Beatitudes ascend from a right love of ourselves, to a right love of our neighbors, to a right love of God.

We can also see an order of the Beatitudes if we consider the rewards promised:

Theirs is the kingdom of heaven

They will be comforted

They will inherit the land

They will be satisfied

They will be shown mercy

They will see God

They will be called children of God

Theirs is the kingdom of heaven

Here we see an ascending order of rewards, in which each reward is better than the previous one. The first three rewards pertain to the *private good* of the person who receives it. To the poor will be given the kingdom of heaven, that is, the possessions of the heavenly realm in exchange for letting go of their earthly possessions: "Sell what you possess and give to the poor, and you will have treasure in heaven" (Matt. 19:21). To those who mourn will be given spiritual consolations instead of earthly consolations. To those who are meek and do not get angry over the loss of their earthly inheritance will be given a resurrected body, an eternal inheritance of the land: "My chosen shall inherit it, and my servants shall dwell there" (Isa. 65:9). Thus, Jesus preferred not to divide the inheritance for the man who was angry at his brother over that inheritance (Luke 12).

The next two rewards pertain to the *common good* of those who are saved. To those who hunger for justice, perfect justice will be given. Thus, they will live in perfect harmony among their fellow servants in heaven. To the merciful, perfect mercy will be shown. Thus, in heaven, their fellow servants shall forgive all the sins of their past life. Stephen shall live in perfect harmony with Paul and will forgive all his transgressions.

Finally, the last three rewards promise the *ultimate common good, namely God*.[16] To the pure of heart, the vision of God will be given, a vision that they shall share in common with all the elect. The peacemakers will be adopted as God's children and conformed to Christ the natural Son of God. Thus, not only will they see God, but they will see God as beloved children behold their Father. Last of all, to the persecuted the kingdom of God will be given. That is, they will be united to God not merely as individuals, or as members of a family, but as citizens of a *kingdom*. And just as the goods of the family exceed the goods of the individual, so do the goods of the kingdom exceed the goods of the family.[17]

At first glance, the last reward looks identical to the first reward, since both are expressed in the same words "kingdom of heaven." But notice that Jesus calls twice-blessed the one who practices this last Beatitude, and he places special emphasis upon it. So it is unlikely that Jesus simply intends to signify the exact same reward in the exact same way in the first and last Beatitudes. I think it is better to interpret this last reward as referring to the principal part of the kingdom of God, namely, the King himself. According to this interpretation, the reward of the first Beatitude refers to the extrinsic elements that are the created goods of the kingdom of heaven, whereas the last Beatitude first of all refers to the uncreated source of the kingdom, God himself, understood as a good common to all the citizens of heaven.

Even if the rewards promised by the first and last Beatitude are different in content, yet the fact that they share the same name indicates that there is a kind of circle in the Beatitudes (the last shall be first, and the first shall be last). This signifies many things. First of all, it represents the completeness and exhaustiveness of the Beatitudes, since it signifies that they embrace every good necessary for perfect happiness. Secondly, it represents the eternal nature of the reward, since a circle has no beginning or end, like eternity. Furthermore, that the eighth reward bears the same name as the first calls to mind the seven days of the week of creation, in which the first and the eighth day bear the same name. For just as on the first day God said *let there be light*, so on the eighth day, the day of Jesus' Resurrection, God once again says it. Finally, it represents the fact that all of the Beatitudes are somehow connected and form a unity, just as one who travels upon a circle ends where he began. For just as the interval of the octave in music is in some way the same note, uniting all the intermediate notes, so also the first and eighth Beatitudes are in some way one and unite all of the intermediate Beatitudes.

So far, we have seen that there is an order among the Beatitudes on the part of the reasons for merit (the first half of each Beatitude), and on the part of the rewards promised (the second half of each Beatitude). But there is also an interesting parallel between the order of the Beatitudes and the progression of the life of Christ.

Christ was born poor and died persecuted for the sake of righteousness. In between, especially throughout the different stages of his passion, we find that Jesus lived these Beatitudes perfectly, and in the same order in which he taught them. For in the garden of Gethsemane, Jesus sorrowed (Matt. 26:38). As he was brought before unjust judges such as Caiaphas and Pontius Pilate, he remained silent and meek. On the cross, he thirsted, and he showed mercy to his murderers: "Father, forgive them, for they know not what they do" (Luke 23:34). Throughout the entire time of his passion, Jesus remained pure in heart, never becoming bitter or returning insult for insult: "When he was insulted, he

THE KIND OF HAPPINESS PROMISED

returned no insult; when he suffered, he did not threaten; instead, he handed himself over to the one who judges justly" (1 Pet. 2:23, NAB). Finally, by his death he made peace between heaven and earth, between Jew and Gentile: "making peace by the blood of his cross" (Col. 1:20). So the order of the Beatitudes also reflects the life of Christ, who both taught and lived according to what he taught.

Why do so many of the Beatitudes speak about painful experiences like poverty, sadness, hunger, and persecution, and how are these reconcilable with being perfectly happy?

No one imagines heaven as a place where everyone is poor, sad, hungry, and persecuted. So if these Beatitudes are attempting to portray a picture of perfect happiness, it seems they aren't doing a very good job. To call the Beatitudes counterintuitive is an understatement. In fact, some of them seem to be the very antithesis of happiness. How can we explain this?

To begin, Jesus needs to speak in very stark terms in order to free us from our false views about happiness. The Catholic author Flannery O'Connor once gave an illuminating explanation why so many of her works included such grotesque and violent elements:

> When you can assume your audience holds the same beliefs you do, you can relax and use more normal means of talking to it; when you have to assume that it does not, then you have to make your vision apparent by shock—to the hard of hearing you shout, and for the almost-blind you draw large and startling figures.[18]

Modern man is practically deaf and blind to fundamental moral realities, so she had to shout and startle. The people to whom Jesus addresses his Beatitudes are also among the nearly deaf and almost blind, so he has to startle us. Jesus knew that if he described happiness in terms that we could possibly interpret as allowing for us to cling to our love for this world, we would have twisted his words until we convinced ourselves that he was saying we could love everything this world has to offer and still love the Father.

Even though Jesus has told us that it is very difficult for the rich to be saved, still most Christians desire wealth. Imagine if Jesus had said, "So long as you love wealth in the right way, you can be saved." Would there be anyone who took a vow of poverty based upon such a teaching? So Jesus states as clearly as possible that happiness does not consist in the goods this world has to offer; in fact, it somehow consists in the *opposite* of what this world has to offer.

In the introduction, I offered a metaphor that describes the condition of our fallen race in its search for happiness. We are like flies on a windowsill trying to get out into the light, but we are unable to get to the light because we keep bumping into the glass. The way out into the light is right behind us, but we have to go through the darkness to get there. If we follow our fallen instincts, we are condemned to seeking happiness in vain, and like the fly we will simply die on the windowsill. But if we will follow Jesus through the darkness, through poverty and sadness, hunger, thirst, and persecution, we will find our way into the light.

Moreover, our human nature has been wounded deeply by original sin. One of the effects of this wound is that we are inclined to love lesser goods much more than greater goods. I like to give the example of a three-year-old child who is given a choice between a bowl of ice cream and a fully-paid-for college education. The three-year-old will choose the ice cream every time. Original sin makes us like that child with regard to happiness. We feel convinced that having riches and bodily comforts and human esteem are the primary components of happiness. In fact, they are not essential causes of happiness, and we find sufficient evidence for this among the very rich: their lives tend to be more miserable than the lives of others. Happiness is an acquired taste, and we need to habituate ourselves to loving the better goods more than the lesser goods. All the while, to do this we must fight against the inclinations of original sin.

Finally, we have to remember that the painful experiences Jesus describes are due to some lack in a created good that is *passing away.* These are goods we will have to lose anyway, so there is no sense in pretending that we will be happy if we possess them. A "happiness" that has a time limit is no happiness at all. It is more a source of anxiety at the impending loss than a source of peace and joy. In contrast, the person who has interiorly renounced these goods, and seen them for what they truly are—mere signs of our Father's love for us (and inadequate signs at that)—will have a lasting joy in God himself and the goods that shall not pass away. This sentiment is expressed well in a passage from the prophet Habakkuk:

> For though the fig tree blossom not nor fruit be on the vines, though the yield of the olive fail and the terraces produce no nourishment, though the flocks disappear from the fold and there be no herd in the stalls, yet will I rejoice in the Lord and exult in my saving God. God, my Lord, is my strength; he makes my feet swift as those of hinds and enables me to go upon the heights (3:17–19, NAB).

Habakkuk is expressing in summary form what ought to have been the attitude of God's people during their entire journey from the land of Egypt to the Promised Land. During that journey, God was often giving his people the bare minimum of comfort: just enough food, water, and shelter. Often God brought them to the point of utter destitution and even starvation, yet at these times he miraculously gave them what they needed, and sometimes much more. But they wanted to have more comfort, more than just the manna and water from the rock, and were willing to pay the price of slavery to do it: "Would that we had meat for food! Oh, how well off we were in Egypt!" (Num. 11:18, NAB).

What God did for the Israelites in the desert, he does also for his chosen ones: he often brings us to the point where we cannot go on because of such a shortage of created goods, yet he constantly intervenes by miraculously providing just enough for us to go on. God does this so that we can have a relationship of constant trust in him, lest we trust in the goods of this world instead. The greatest danger of having an abundance of created goods is that we cease to see our lives as completely dependent upon the care and providence of our heavenly Father.

It is true that in heaven, we will not experience any kind of pain, whether physical or spiritual. These evils of poverty, sadness, hunger, thirst, and persecution will no longer be our lot in heaven. This is why the Beatitudes speak of a reward in the future. Nevertheless, if we love God and the things of God as we ought, even in this life we will consider the loss of these goods as insignificant in comparison to the joys for which we hope. And unless we learn to love God above all things, and all things for God's sake, we shall never find true happiness. This is the message of the Beatitudes.

3

THE FIRST BEATITUDE

THE POOR IN SPIRIT

Better is a poor man who walks in his integrity than a rich man who is perverse in his ways (Prov. 28:6).

Now that we have asked and answered some general questions that pertain to all of the Beatitudes, we turn to consider each Beatitude in particular. For each Beatitude I will ask, usually in this order:[19]

1) Who are those identified as the inheritors of the Beatitude?

2) What is the reward promised for them and why is it appropriate?

3) How can we overcome difficulties in living out this Beatitude?

4) How do Christ and the saints exemplify this Beatitude?

5) To which gift and petition of the Our Father does this correspond?

I will also ask other questions that are specific to each Beatitude.

The first Beatitude is *Blessed are the poor in spirit, for theirs is the kingdom of heaven*. Therefore, I will ask: 1) Who are the poor in spirit? 2) Why is "the kingdom of heaven" an appropriate reward for them? 3) How can we overcome the difficulties in living out poverty of spirit? 4) How did Christ and the saints exemplify this Beatitude? 5) To which gift and petition of the Our Father does it correspond? and 6) Why is this Beatitude first?

Who are the poor in spirit?

We all know what it means to be poor. A poor person lives day-by-day and does not have an abundance of possessions saved up for the future. Each day, a poor person needs to earn or receive the things he needs to survive for that day. His life and work are concerned with necessities: food, clothing, and shelter. He does not have time or money for vacations and pleasant diversions. If someone is particularly poor, he will sometimes even lack necessities for a time. The life of a poor man is summed up well by the proverb: "The poor man toils as his livelihood diminishes, and when he rests he becomes needy" (Sir. 31:4).

So we know who the poor are, but who are the poor *in spirit*? Someone poor in spirit is someone who lives in his spiritual life the way a man who is poor in body lives in his physical life. The physically poor man works each day to receive his bread. The spiritually poor man prays each day to receive spiritual nourishment from the Lord: "Give us this day our daily bread." The physically poor man does not have time for unnecessary distractions. The spiritually poor man sees that he must always attend to the necessities of the spiritual life: prayer, works of mercy, confession of sins, and he does not give in to unnecessary distractions. The physically poor man sometimes lacks even necessary food for a time; the spiritually poor man will sometimes feel abandoned by God and desolation in prayer, yet all the while will continue trusting in his heavenly Father to provide for him.

Another possible meaning for the expression "poor in spirit" is that it names those who are detached from wealth because of their love for God. Someone can be detached from wealth for many reasons. He may be lazy or imprudent; he may be subject to a false ideology that says wealth itself is an evil. None of these exhibit special merit. But those who are detached from wealth because they are attached to God deserve some reward. Such people see money as merely a means to the end of loving God. They freely bestow from their goods upon the poor. They do not sin in order to acquire or keep wealth.

But even among those who are detached from wealth, there are two kinds. First, there are those who are not excessively attached to their wealth so that they rightly subordinate their desire for wealth to the love of God. Second, and more perfectly, there are those whose love for God is so great that they simply have no desire for wealth at all, and even spurn it. Souls such as St. Francis of Assisi exemplify this more perfect poverty of spirit. This kind of poverty of spirit is clearly motivated by the gifts of the Holy Spirit.

In another sense, the poor in spirit can refer to those who are detached from worldly honors. That is, they are humble. And when their poverty of spirit is great, they even spurn worldly honor, as Queen Esther did: "You know that I hate the glory of the pagans . . . that I abhor the sign of grandeur which rests on my head when I appear in public; abhor it like a polluted rag, and do not wear it in private" (Esther 4C:26-27, NAB).

Finally, the expression "poor in spirit" can mean poor in *the Spirit*. This does not mean that they have little or nothing of the Holy Spirit. Rather it means that their poverty is motivated by the indwelling of the Holy Spirit. For such men, the gifts of the Holy Spirit incline them to seek their treasure in heaven: "Sell all that you have and distribute to the poor, and you will have treasure in heaven" (Luke 18:22).

In short, the poor in spirit are those who are humble, those who depend upon God completely for every good bodily and spiritual.

All of these ways of understanding the expression *poor in spirit* have three qualities in common: they all trust in God to provide for their needs; they all are detached from wealth or honor; and they all love God more than wealth or honor. Whoever has these qualities is an inheritor of the kingdom of heaven.

Why does Luke simply say, "Blessed are you poor"?

Luke, when recounting this Beatitude, omits "in spirit," leaving the reader with the impression that poverty by itself is sufficient to inherit the kingdom of heaven. Does Luke disagree with Matthew? Of course, one scriptural text must be interpreted in light of and in harmony with the rest of Scripture. So any explanation of these texts that asserts a contradiction is not a Catholic interpretation, nor is it consistent with the divine authorship of all Scripture.

Nevertheless, there is a reason for the differences among parallel passages. Recall that Luke is recounting the Beatitudes as addressed to the crowds who were following Jesus. These people were extremely poor, and many were considered cursed by God and outcasts by the ruling society in Jerusalem. The very fact that they were following Jesus and attracted to his message was a sign that they had the right

interior dispositions.[20] Jesus perceived their good dispositions, and when he addressed them he wanted to leave them
without any doubt that they were blessed in the eyes of God,
despite their culture telling them that the rich were blessed
by God and the poor were cursed. So Jesus simply says to
them, "Blessed are you poor."

Notice too that, in Luke's account, Jesus uses the second
person ("you") rather than the third person ("those"). This is
because Jesus is speaking directly to the poor right in front of
him. And he knew that they were also poor in spirit, so he
had no need to add this further qualifier "in spirit." Moreover,
by simply saying "poor" Jesus emphasizes simultaneously that
wealth, in itself, is not a sign of God's favor and that poverty of
spirit is more easily achieved by those who are actually poor.

Pope St. Leo the Great explains:

> It would perhaps be doubtful what poor he was speak-
> ing of, if in saying "blessed are the poor" he had added
> nothing which would explain the sort of poor: and then
> that poverty by itself would appear sufficient to win the
> kingdom of heaven which many suffer from hard and
> heavy necessity. But when he says, "Blessed are the poor
> in spirit," he shows that the kingdom of heaven must be
> assigned to those who are recommended by the humility
> of their spirits rather than by the smallness of their means.
> Yet it cannot be doubted that this possession of humility
> is more easily acquired by the poor than the rich.[21]

But isn't wealth a blessing and a sign of God's favor, as happened with Abraham?

All created goods can be considered a blessing from God,
but some created goods, like wealth, are blessings only in

a relative sense. Wealth is a blessing in some circumstances, but not in others. A sign of this is that God always takes away wealth at the end of our lives. As the old adage says, "You can't take it with you!" Everyone dies like a Carthusian. In fact, the case of Abraham is an excellent example that illustrates how someone with wealth can be poor in spirit. The account of Abraham and Lot found in Genesis illustrates how the desire for wealth can be an impediment to spiritual growth. As we read in Genesis 13, both Abraham and Lot came to be very wealthy, and the land could not support both their herds, so their herdsmen began to fight over the shortage of land:

> But Lot also, who was with Abram, had flocks of sheep and herds of beast and tents. Neither was the land able to bear them, that they might dwell together. For their substance was great, and they could not dwell together. Whereupon, also there arose a strife between the herdsmen of Abram and of Lot . . . Abram therefore said to Lot: "Let there be no quarrel, I beseech you, between me and you, and between my herdsmen and your herdsmen. For we are brethren. Behold, the whole land is before you. Depart from me I petition you. If you will go to the left hand, I will take the right. If you choose the right hand, I will pass to the left." And Lot, lifting up his eyes, saw all the country of the Jordan, which was watered throughout, before the Lord destroyed Sodom and Gomorrah, as the paradise of the Lord, and like Egypt as one comes to Segor. And Lot chose to himself the country about the Jordan, and he departed from the east. And they were separated: one brother from the other. Abram dwelt in the land of Canaan, and Lot abode in the towns that were about the Jordan, and dwelt in Sodom (Gen. 13:5–12, DRA).

One of the most striking things about this passage is how frequently it repeats that, on account of their material possessions, two close relatives had to live apart from one another. Material goods are the least of all goods because they can be exhausted by a single individual. If I am going to eat this piece of pizza, you can't eat it; when I am wearing my socks you can't wear them. Material goods either cannot be shared at all or they are divided and diminished when they are shared. And so material or temporal possessions are often the cause of strife, even between family members. And they often cause people to give up greater goods for the sake of lesser goods. Undoubtedly, love and living together with those whom we love is a greater good than any material possession. Yet, as the passage from Genesis states, "They were separated: one brother from another."

This theme of material goods separating brothers is found many times in Scripture. For example, in Luke's Gospel, the parable of the prodigal son speaks about how the inheritance divided the older and younger son from each other and from their father. And in the middle of Luke 12 a young man comes to Jesus saying: "Teacher, bid my brother divide the inheritance with me" (v.13). How often as a priest have I encountered family members fighting over their inheritance and refusing to love one another for the sake of the love they have for money? I even know of a case of a man who wanted his mother to leave his inheritance to his live-in girlfriend to avoid paying his back taxes. When his mother refused, he never spoke to her again for the rest of her life. He preferred his love of money to the love of his own mother; and for the rest of his life he bore in his heart the shame of it.

A second thing about this text is that although Abraham is completely detached from his wealth (as evidenced by his willingness to let Lot choose where to live, and later his willingness to sacrifice even his beloved son Isaac), Lot is still very attached to his wealth. He sees the green, well-watered lands around Sodom and Gomorrah and is willing to live among the Sodomites for the sake of his possessions. He forsakes the companionship of his virtuous kinsmen and chooses to dwell with vicious men merely to keep possession of his wealth. Later on, Lot's attachment to things of this world will cost him dearly.

Both Lot and Abraham were righteous men and pleasing to God: they both loved God above all things. St. Peter says of Lot that he was righteous, and that he was tormented by the wickedness of his neighbors (2 Pet. 2:7). But the difference between them was that Abraham loved God above all things *and he loved all things for God's sake*, even his beloved son. Lot, on the other hand, did not love all things for God's sake, even if he loved God more than those things. Lot was someone who was still attached to his wealth. Even when God sent his angels to rescue Lot and his family from destruction, he remained attached. We read that "as he lingered, they took his hand and the hand of his wife and of his two daughters, because the Lord spared him" (Gen. 19:16, DRA). Even when threatened with destruction, Lot's attachments nearly proved fatal, but by the mercy of God, the angels dragged him and his family out by force!

What was the result of this difference in their loves? Whereas Abraham's love had the power to save those who were dearest to him, Lot's love was strong enough only to obtain his own salvation. As Peter says, "If the righteous man is scarcely saved, where will the impious and sinner appear?" (1 Pet. 4:18). Abraham's love was powerful enough to save Lot, but Lot's love was not sufficient to procure the salvation of his wife. We too must recognize that it is not enough to love God above all things and then just take advantage of all the goods of this world that are licit. If we cling to our wealth and try to find happiness both in the next life and here below, perhaps we ourselves will scarcely be saved by God's mercy, but we will not have the power by our lives or by our prayers to save those whom we love. We must not cling to wealth. Instead, we must love all things for God's sake. This is why the Lord pronounces the woes in addition to the Beatitudes: to impress upon us the radical decision we must make to place all our hope in God and in the goods of the world to come.

Why is "the kingdom of heaven" an appropriate reward for the poor in spirit?

To those who are poor in spirit, a kingdom is promised. It makes intuitive sense that those who most deserve wealth are those who are least attached to it. And what could bring greater wealth than to inherit an entire kingdom? We read in the Gospel according to Luke that as a reward for using their master's wealth well, his servants were given authority over many cities (Luke 19). The implication is that if someone governs his possessions as if he were the steward of another, he proves himself worthy to govern even greater possessions. And the greatest possession of all seems to be an entire kingdom.

But the meaning of the term *kingdom,* as it is used here, must be clarified. Sometimes a kingdom refers to the king and subjects together, but sometimes a kingdom refers just to those things that are under the authority of the king. I think that in this Beatitude, it is the latter meaning of kingdom that is primarily being used. For it is appropriate for one who has governed his God-given possessions well to receive greater possessions from God. Thus, as I mentioned already, to the poor will be given the kingdom of heaven, that is, the possessions of the heavenly realm, in exchange for letting go of their earthly possessions: "Sell what you possess and give to the poor, and you will have treasure in heaven" (Matt. 19:21). So *kingdom of heaven* here is distinguished from the meaning of kingdom of heaven that is the reward for the final (eighth) Beatitude; the reward of the first Beatitude refers to the extrinsic elements that are the created goods of the kingdom of heaven, whereas the last Beatitude seems to refer primarily to the uncreated source of the kingdom, the King himself.

Three dangers of wealth

Scripture reveals three distinct dangers associated with the wealth. The first danger is that we love wealth so much that we are willing to do injustice to others in order to possess and increase it. St. James speaks of this danger when he writes:

> Come now, you rich, weep and howl for the miseries that are coming upon you. Your riches have rotted and your garments are moth-eaten. Your gold and silver have rusted, and their rust will be evidence against you and will eat your flesh like fire. You have laid up treasure for the last days. Behold, the wages of the laborers who mowed your fields, which you kept back by fraud, cry out; and the cries of the harvesters have reached the ears of the Lord of hosts (James 5:1–4).

This is the most serious and wicked moral state associated with the love of wealth, and so it bears the greatest punishment. The punishment will be in very proportion to the wealth such a person has amassed.

The second danger is that we love our wealth so much that we are unwilling to part with it even when someone nearby is in serious need. This is described by Jesus in the parable about Lazarus and the rich man:

There was a rich man, who was clothed in purple and fine linen and who feasted sumptuously every day. And at his gate lay a poor man named Lazarus, full of sores, who desired to be fed with what fell from the rich man's table; moreover the dogs came and licked his sores. The poor man died and was carried by the angels to Abraham's bosom. The rich man also died and was buried; and in Hades, being in torment, he lifted up his eyes, and saw Abraham far off and Lazarus in his bosom. And he called out, "Father Abraham, have mercy upon me, and send Lazarus to dip the end of his finger in water and cool my tongue; for I am in anguish in this flame." But Abraham said, "Son, remember that you in your lifetime received your good things, and Lazarus in like manner evil things; but now he is comforted here, and you are in anguish. And besides all this, between us and you a great chasm has been fixed, in order that those who would pass from here to you may not be able, and none may cross from there to us." And he said, "Then, I beg you, father, to send him to my father's house, for I have five brothers, so that he may warn them, lest they also come into this place of torment." But Abraham said, "They have Moses and the prophets; let them hear them." And he said, "No, father Abraham; but if someone goes to them from the dead, they will re-pent." He said to him, "If they do not hear Moses and the prophets, neither will they be convinced if someone should rise from the dead" (Luke 16:19–31).

In this account, the rich man is not accused of stealing or somehow acquiring his wealth through injustice. His sin is rather that he had an overabundance of wealth and did not share it with someone in dire need who was at his very gate. He was not so attached to his wealth that he would steal to get it, but he was so attached to it that he would not give it up even out of love for his neighbor. This defect is more common than the first among those who call themselves Christians.

The third danger, by far the most subtle and far-reaching, is using our wealth as a substitute for God's providence. Jesus speaks of this in the twelfth chapter of Luke's Gospel:

One of the multitude said to him, "Teacher, bid my brother divide the inheritance with me." But he said to him, "Man, who made me a judge or divider over you?" And he said to them, "Take heed, and beware of all covetousness; for a man's life does not consist in the abundance of his possessions." And he told them a parable, saying, "The land of a rich man brought forth plentifully; and he thought to himself, 'What shall I do, for I have nowhere to store my crops?' And he said, 'I will do this: I will pull down my barns, and build larger ones; and there I will store all my grain and my goods. And I will say to my soul, "Soul, you have ample goods laid up for many years; take your ease, eat, drink, be merry."' But God said to him, 'Fool! This night your soul is required of you; and the things you have prepared, whose will they be?' So is he who lays up treasure for himself, and is not rich toward God" (12:13–21).

The rich man in this parable is not accused of stealing. His wealth comes simply from his own crops and land. Neither is he accused of lacking generosity with someone nearby who is in need, as was the rich man in the previous parable.

Rather, the sin of this man is that he "lays up treasure for himself and is not rich toward God." That is, *he is using his wealth as a substitute for trusting in God's fatherly care.* His wealth is a safety net in case God doesn't provide him with as much as he thinks he needs. And so he is no longer in communion with his Father.

Imagine a family in which one of the children hoards the food that the father daily provides and stores it in his room. Then one day the child stops coming to meals altogether and just stays in his room eating the food he has stored up. This would be an indication of a serious lack of trust in the heart of the child, and a failure to appreciate that this relationship of trust with his father is more important than the food itself. He fears that one day the food will stop appearing on the table, so he makes plans for the doomsday future he has imagined. Put simply, he does not trust that his father will continue to provide for him.

And this is perhaps the greatest danger of wealth for our souls: not injustice, not neglect of the poor, but substituting our wealth for the providence of our Father in heaven. We say to God with our lips, "I trust in you," but then we make a safety net out of our possessions just in case our Father will not catch us when we fall. See how different the life of the poor man is from the life of the rich man. The poor man every day comes to his Father with his hands empty, asking for his daily bread. I cannot help thinking of the beautiful character Tevye from *Fiddler on the Roof.* He was a man in constant communion with God, for he had no other choice. How pleased the Father is that his children come to him trustingly each day, knowing that were it not for him, they could not provide for themselves. But the rich man may pray, "Give us this day our daily bread" yet he knows full well where today's bread is, and tomorrow's bread, and the next day's. For such a one there is no risk, no real need to trust, and hence no deep communion with the Father.

I once read a remarkable story told by a woman named Gloria Polo. She had been struck by lightning, and while she hovered between life and death she had a vision of a man whose prayers saved her soul from damnation. In her account she writes about a poor country farmer in South America who had his small farm raided by soldiers who stole his chickens and burned his crops. And he had nothing left for his family but two bills: one of 5,000 pesos, the other 10,000. But he went to church still giving thanks to God in the midst of his misfortune. And he put into the collection basket the 10,000-peso bill, and with the 5,000 he bought a loaf of bread for his family, trusting that God would take care of him. The bread was wrapped in newspaper, and in the newspaper he read about a woman who had been struck by lightning and was in danger of death. So he prayed for her, and because he was so full of childlike trust, his prayers for the salvation of souls was very powerful in God's sight. To be like this man is to be like a little child who completely depends upon his parents for his every need. In contrast, we can see how covetousness, the attachment to wealth, harms our union with the Father and impedes purity of heart.

Here the question arises: Is it sinful to plan for the future? For example, is it wrong for a man to save money to buy a home or a farm? This seems to be contrary to what is said in Sirach: "God, in the beginning, created man, he made him subject to his own free choice" (Sir. 15:14, NAB). For if we are not permitted to plan for the future and provide for ourselves, it seems that nothing remains for us to do but merely remain inert.

The truth is that God does want us to use the mind he gave us to labor and provide for ourselves and others. And he expects us to take reasonable account of the future in order to do so. We know, for example, that Jesus and his disciples had a common store of money (John 13:29). But we should not do this in the wrong way, as St. James warns in his epistle:

> Come now, you who say, "Today or tomorrow we will go into such and such a town and spend a year there and trade and get gain"; whereas you do not know about tomorrow. What is your life? For you are a mist that appears for a little time and then vanishes. Instead you ought to say, "If the Lord wills, we shall live and we shall do this or that." As it is, you boast in your arrogance. All such boasting is evil (James 4:13–16).

St. Thomas explains this passage:

> Although it is in our power to act, yet it is not in our power that our actions attain to their due ends on account of the impediments which can happen. And so, that which each one attains by his action lies subject to the disposition of the divine [will]. Therefore, the Lord commands us not to be solicitous about those things the care of which pertain to God, namely, the outcomes of our actions. God does not, however, prohibit us to be solicitous about those things which pertain to us, namely about our work . . . Hence, he does not prohibit that we store up those things which are necessary for us tomorrow in their time, but [he prohibits] that we be solicitous about future events with a certain desperation of the divine help, or lest we be preoccupied today with the solicitude which we will have to have tomorrow.[22]

Thus, St. James does not prohibit doing business, or making plans, but rather adds later that our disposition ought to be: "If the Lord will, and if we live, we shall do this or that."

How can we overcome the difficulties in living out poverty of spirit?

There is a special difficulty in living out this Beatitude. The Gospels relate that a rich young man came to Jesus to ask what he must do to be saved. When Jesus invited him to sell all he had and follow him, it says that "he went away sorrowful; for he had great possessions" (Matt. 19:22). Although he had kept all the commandments, he could not inherit beatitude. Instead, his great wealth caused him sorrow. This caused Jesus to remark, "How hard it is for those who trust in riches to enter the kingdom of God! It is easier for a camel to go through the eye of a needle than for a rich man to enter the kingdom of God" (Mark 10:24–25).

It is striking how even in spite of these strong words by our Lord, most who claim to follow Jesus would rather be rich than poor. If Jesus had said, "It is nearly impossible to enter heaven if you are," we would expect that all Christians would avoid and rid themselves altogether of whatever fills in that blank. Yet when it is "riches" that fills in the blank, suddenly everyone has an excuse. I have met many Christians who desire to be wealthy, and very few who desire to be poor. If you looked at the lives of most Christians today, you would think that Jesus had said the opposite of the first Beatitude!

So let us examine each excuse one by one. One person says, "It is no sin to be wealthy! So long as I am not overly attached to my wealth." True, it is no sin to be wealthy. But I ask you this: how many men cling to their wealth with all their might while protesting that they have no attachment to it? They will make the road to heaven nearly impossible for the sake of the wealth they claim to care nothing about. If you care nothing about it, why then do you not cast it off and follow our Lord in the freedom of poverty?

Another excuse for being wealthy runs like this: "It is not for my sake, but for my family, that my children shall be financially secure and not have to worry about money." When your children are wealthy, to them also the words of Jesus will apply: it will be harder for them to enter into the kingdom of God than for a camel to pass through the eye of a needle. By your decision to enrich your children do you want to make your children's salvation nearly impossible? Where you might have enriched your children with an example of virtue and mercy to the poor, you have impoverished them with an example of covetousness and distrust in divine providence!

My own father was a beautiful example for us in this regard. He spent our inheritance on the poor, but he bequeathed to his children a much more precious inheritance: the example of his generosity. In my entire life, I never once saw my father pass a poor man without giving him something. Sometimes, he would be driving his car and on the other side of the street he would see a poor person pushing a shopping cart. And he would make a U-turn just so he could give him something. Once, when I was a teenager, we went to Tijuana, where there is a bridge leading from California to Mexico. And on the Mexican side there are literally hundreds of beggars each holding a cup. And I remember thinking to myself, "Finally, dad is going to pass a poor person without giving him something."

I was wrong. He went to a local bank, cashed a hundred-dollar bill for quarters and filled his pockets with them, then stopped and gave something to every single beggar on that bridge. At the time I was irritated. But now I look back upon my irritation with great compunction, knowing that in all the years that Jesus sat begging in the persons of those poor beggars, he never met a man as generous as my father.

It seems to me that there is only one sound excuse for possessing riches: that one might care for the needs of the poor with his excess, while living modestly oneself, using only what is truly necessary for himself and his family. Men such as these are worthy citizens of the kingdom of God.

When it comes down to it, the great obstacle to living the first Beatitude is fear: Fear that your Father in heaven will not take care of you if you generously share your possessions with others. In order to live this Beatitude fully and joyfully, you must pray for courage and trust.

The example of Christ and the saints

St. Paul says about Christ: "You know the grace of our Lord Jesus Christ, that though he was rich, yet for your sake he became poor, so that by his poverty you might become rich" (2 Cor. 8:9). How did he go from rich to being poor? Paul answers again: "Though he was in the form of God, did not count equality with God a thing to be grasped, but emptied himself, taking the form of a servant, being born in the likeness of men" (Phil. 2:6–7). There is no greater way to manifest a love of poverty than for the Creator to take on the form of a creature. Metaphysically, this is to go from the fullness of being almost to non-being. If a man were voluntarily to become a speck of dust, it would still not compare to what the Son of God has done out of love for us.

Not only that, but once he assumed our human condition, as man he lived in poverty, though he had the choice to live however he pleased. He was born in a stable, lived in an obscure, dusty corner of the Roman Empire, labored with his own hands, and said about himself "the Son of Man has nowhere to lay his head" (Matt 8:20; Luke 9:58). As he traveled along preaching, he lived off the alms of others.

And when he died, he died naked, with even his clothes stripped from his body. All of this he did by choice, for he had the power to lay his life down and to take it up again (John 10:17–18; see John 3:35; Matt. 11:27; and Luke 10:22).

From all this, it is clear that Jesus preferred poverty to riches; that he loved poverty. And in this he was supremely happy. In order to be more like Christ, we should do the same.

St. Francis of Assisi

There are few of whom "blessed are the poor of spirit" can be more truly said than of St. Francis of Assisi. St. Bonaventure wrote in his biography of the saint: "No man was ever so covetous of gold as he of poverty." There is no need to recount in detail how he forsook the wealth of his merchant class parents and how he distributed everything, even his clothes, save a hairshirt. According to one account, when he walked into the snowy forest having dispossessed himself of everything, he began to sing.

In his observance of poverty, St. Francis was unbending. On one occasion, when the brethren were so poor there was not enough to supply even necessities, his vicar suggested that perhaps some of the novices could bring some part of their possessions with them to the community. To this, Francis responded that he would first strip the altar of the Blessed Virgin Mary, for "the Blessed Virgin would rather see her altar unadorned and the counsel of the holy Gospel perfectly observed, than that the altar should be ornamented and the counsel of her son set at naught."

But in all of this, from beginning to end, St. Francis was joyful in his poverty, or rather we should say, because of it. The words of G.K. Chesterton from his biography of Francis aptly express the joy that accompanied the saint's poverty:

He plunged after poverty as men have dug madly for gold. And it is precisely the positive and passionate quality of this part of his personality which is a challenge to the modern mind . . . It is certain that he held on this heroic or unnatural course from the moment when he went forth in his hair-shirt into the winter woods to the moment when he desired even in his death agony to lie bare upon the bare ground, to prove that he had and that he was nothing. And we can say with almost as deep a certainty that the stars that passed above that gaunt and wasted corpse stark upon the rocky floor had for once, in all their shining cycles round the world of laboring humanity, looked down upon a happy man.

To which gift and petition of the Our Father does this Beatitude correspond?

It is the teaching of many Fathers and Doctors of the Church (for example, St. Augustine and St. Thomas Aquinas) that each Beatitude corresponds to a gift of the Holy Spirit and a petition of the Our Father (the eighth Beatitude is a special case, as we shall see later). That each Beatitude should correspond to a gift of the Holy Spirit is clear if we understand that each Beatitude is the activity proceeding from each gift.[23] This is similar to the way that an activity proceeds from a habit such as a virtue. In the same way that just actions flow from the virtue of justice, and generous actions flow from the virtue of generosity, the Beatitudes flow from the gifts of the Holy Spirit. But it is not as clear that there should be a Beatitude corresponding to each petition of the Our Father.

The Our Father is the perfect summary of prayer, and prayer is founded upon the theological virtue of hope:

"Prayer is recommended to men, that by it they may obtain from God what they hope to secure from him."[24] As we have already seen, the joy of the Beatitudes is present already in this life precisely through this virtue of hope. Therefore, corresponding to the things of heaven that we hope to obtain by prayer are the Beatitudes we already begin to experience in this life through hope.

So, to which gift and petition does "blessed are the poor in spirit" correspond? The poor in spirit are humble and detached from earthly riches and honors. And this attitude of detachment belongs to every virtuous person. But the gifts of the Holy Spirit go beyond what is virtuous. Someone acting by the gifts of the Holy Spirit is not only detached from wealth and honors; he positively spurns them lest they form in any way an obstacle between him and God. This disposition is produced by the fear that heavenly goods should be lost if earthly goods are gained, since the Lord has taught us how difficult it is for the rich to enter the kingdom of God. And, therefore, through the gift of fear of the Lord, the soul submits to the yoke of the divine counsel and becomes poor in spirit. In keeping with this, Augustine teaches:

> The Beatitudes begin with humility: "Blessed are the poor in spirit," that is, those not puffed up, while the soul submits itself to divine authority, fearing lest after this life it go away to punishment, although perhaps in this life it might seem to itself to be happy.[25]

A little further on he adds: "The fear of God corresponds to the humble, of whom it is here said, 'Blessed are the poor in spirit,' that is, those not puffed up, not proud: to whom the apostle (St. Paul) says, 'Be not high-minded, but fear.'"[26]

Since this fear of the Lord is the gift corresponding to the Beatitude "blessed are the poor in spirit," and because it is precisely this fear by which we revere God's holiness, it is evident that this Beatitude also corresponds to the petition "hallowed be thy name." Thus, St. Thomas teaches: "If fear of the Lord is that by which the poor in spirit are blessed, we also beseech that the name of God be hallowed among men by chaste fear."[27] This reverence for God is the beginning of the spiritual life, and so rightly corresponds to the first of the Beatitudes.

Why is this Beatitude first?

The final question that naturally arises regarding this Beatitude is: Why is it first? One reason is because in all times of human history, the rich are most of all thought to be happy—by the world and by human standards. This was so true in Jesus' time that being rich was considered a sign of God's favor and being poor a sign of God's displeasure. This explains why even the apostles marveled at Jesus' claim that it was very hard for the rich to be saved. They respond, "Then who can be saved?" (Matt. 19:25; Mark 10:26; Luke 18:26). So the very first thing Jesus wants to make clear is that the poor are, in fact, *favored* by God: "Blessed are the poor."

A second reason why this Beatitude is first is because it is the easiest to practice, and hence practicing this Beatitude is a preparation for practicing the other Beatitudes. External goods are less connected to us than the goods of our bodies or the goods of our souls. Hence, we can give up these external goods with less suffering than the goods of the body or soul. If someone asked you whether you would rather have a lot of money or your health, you would certainly answer that health is more important.

Finally, this Beatitude is first because it requires the least spiritual maturity to practice. It takes very little spiritual maturity to see that wealth cannot be our happiness. Money is always a means to something else, whereas happiness is the ultimate end of all our desires and choices. (It is harder to see that, for example, emotional satisfaction is not our happiness.) Hence, the Beatitudes "blessed are those who mourn" and "blessed are the meek" require greater spiritual maturity to practice than this one. It is to these Beatitudes that we turn our attention next.

4

THE THIRD BEATITUDE

THOSE WHO MOURN

It is better to go to the house of mourning than to go to the
house of feasting; for this is the end of all men, and the
living will lay it to heart. Sorrow is better than laughter, for
by sadness of countenance the heart is made glad. The heart
of the wise is in the house of mourning; but the heart of
fools is in the house of mirth (Eccles. 7:2–4).

After pronouncing the poor to be blessed, the Lord next dares
to proclaim that even those who mourn and who are meek
are blessed. Whereas the Beatitude about poverty concerns
external goods, the Beatitudes about meekness and mourning concern the *dispositions of the sense appetites*, so that these
Beatitudes touch upon a more interior and intimate aspect of
human nature. There is a Beatitude directed to the *concupis-*
cible appetite (blessed are those who mourn) and a Beatitude
directed to the *irascible* appetite (blessed are the meek).[28]

The second Beatitude is perhaps the most difficult to understand, since, on the face of it, it contains a contradiction: happy are those who are sad. Therefore, some distinctions are in order if we are going to understand and practice this Beatitude.

If human nature were simple without any division in the human soul, it would be impossible for a man to both rejoice and mourn. But human nature is not simple. The human soul has a lower part and a higher part. St. Paul refers to this distinction when he writes about "spirit and soul and body" (1 Thess. 5:23). The "spirit" is the higher power and the "soul" is the lower power. Thus it is possible to rejoice in the spirit while mourning in the soul. So St. Thomas asserts about Christ's soul:

> In Christ's soul there followed joy from the vision of God and the pain of the passion from the feeling of injury . . . the higher and the lower appetite could be affected in different ways, so that the higher would rejoice and the lower fear or grieve, as happens in one who hopes to get health from some horrible remedy.[29]

Rejoicing in the spirit, the higher power of the soul, while sorrowing in the lower power of the soul: this is how we can be happy when we mourn.

Who are those who mourn?

The first question we must answer is who is Jesus identifying as "those who mourn"? The Greek word used by Matthew, *penthountes,* does not just mean sorrowing; more specifically, it means a *mourning of one who has died.* This gives us insight into the precise meaning intended by Jesus. The sorrow here has a connection with death.

Now, there are many who mourn the loss of a loved one, and although this is natural, it is not in itself meritorious. For there are many who mourn excessively or out of self-interest. Therefore, the kind of mourning that is the lot of the whole human race, believers and unbelievers alike, does not make someone blessed. This is what Pope Leo the Great teaches:

> This mourning, beloved, to which eternal comforting is promised is not the same as the affliction of this world: nor do those laments which are poured out in the sorrowings of the whole human race make anyone blessed. The reason for holy groanings, the cause of blessed tears, is very different.[30]

Thus, we must distinguish between worldly sorrow and holy sorrow: "For godly sorrow produces a salutary repentance without regret, but worldly sorrow produces death" (2 Cor. 7:10, NAB).

One way in which we can mourn death in a holy and meritorious way is by mourning over a deceased loved one with hope and faith in the resurrection of the dead promised by Christ. It was in this way that Martha mourned over her brother Lazarus:

> Jesus said to her: "Your brother will rise again." Martha said to him: "I know that he will rise again in the resurrection at the last day." Jesus said to her: "I am the resurrection and the life; he who believes in me, though he die, yet shall he live, and whoever lives and believes in me shall never die. Do you believe this?" She said to him: "Yes, Lord; I believe that you are the Christ, the Son of God, he who is coming into the world" (John 11:23–27).

Jesus rewards Martha's faith by raising her brother to life again even in this life as a sign that he would raise him to everlasting glory at the last day. And so, one might say that Martha inherited something of the reward promised by this Beatitude early.

A second way we can mourn in a meritorious way is by voluntarily accepting the pain and suffering that come with putting our old self to death. Thus Paul commands us, "Put to death, then, the parts of you that are earthly: immorality, impurity, passion, evil desire, and the greed that is idolatry" (Col. 3:5, NAB). This death is first begun in us sacramentally in baptism, but is brought to perfection through our own choices to prefer spiritual and heavenly goods to earthly ones. Paul describes this attitude elsewhere when he says,

> I even consider everything as a loss because of the supreme good of knowing Christ Jesus my Lord. For his sake I have accepted the loss of all things and I consider them so much rubbish, that I may gain Christ and be found in him, not having any righteousness of my own based on the law but that which comes through faith in Christ, the righteousness from God, depending on faith to know him and the power of his resurrection and the sharing of his sufferings by being conformed to his death, if somehow I may attain the resurrection from the dead (Phil. 3:8–11, NAB).

In another way, we mourn death in a meritorious way when we mourn the spiritual death of ourselves or others who sin. The scriptures speak of death both in a physical sense and in a spiritual sense. Thus, God says to Adam, "But of the tree of the knowledge of good and evil you shall not eat, for in the day that you eat of it you shall die" (Gen. 2:17). Yet Adam did not die physically on that day, but rather spiritually. And St. John says simply, "He who does not love remains in death" (1 John 3:14). This spiritual death happens whenever someone commits a serious sin: "There is sin which is mortal" (1 John 5:16). And, therefore, it is right to be saddened over that spiritual death brought about by mortal sin, as Paul mourns over the Corinthians who sinned (2 Cor. 12:21). Thus, Pope St. Leo the Great writes:

> Religious grief mourns sin (either that of another or one's own) nor does it mourn for that which is wrought by God's justice, but it laments over that which is committed by man's iniquity, where he that does wrong is more to be deplored than he who suffers it. Because the unjust man's wrongdoing plunges him into punishment, but the just man's endurance leads him on to glory.[31]

St. James recommends this kind of mourning in response to one's own sins: "Cleanse your hands, you sinners, and purify your hearts, you of two minds. Begin to lament, to mourn, to weep. Let your laughter be turned into mourning and your joy into dejection. Humble yourselves before the Lord and he will exalt you" (James 4:8–10, NAB).

Finally, we mourn meritoriously when we *mourn the death of Jesus*. For it was on account of our sins that Jesus had to die. And by sorrowing over his death, we make reparation for its cause. St. Alphonsus Liguori quotes St. Bonaventure approvingly when he writes, "He who desires to go on advancing from virtue to virtue, from grace to grace, should meditate continually on the Passion of Jesus. And there is no practice more profitable for the entire sanctification of the soul than the frequent meditation on the sufferings of Jesus Christ."[32]

Yet, why does Jesus tell the women on the Way of the Cross, "Daughters of Jerusalem, do not weep for me" (Luke 23:28)? Because they were weeping for him as though for a common criminal, not as over a just man unjustly condemned to death. For certainly Jesus would not have corrected them if they were doing a good deed. But the truth was that they ought to have wept more over their own sins that caused his death and over the punishment due to their sins more than over the sufferings of his punishment.

A beautiful way to mourn the death of Jesus well is to meditate on the sorrowful mysteries of the rosary, or to pray the Stations of the Cross, or even just to meditate upon a crucifix. All of these ways of mourning will make us blessed.

Why is the reward "they will be consoled" appropriate?

Consolation is the assistance one receives from another to overcome sorrow. Thus, it is appropriate that consolation should be the reward for those who sorrow in a meritorious way. The appropriateness of this reward is made even clearer when we understand that the specific sorrow of this Beatitude is a mourning over death. We mourn over death because in death we have been separated from one whom we love. The perfect remedy for this is to be united with one whom we love.

Anyone who has experienced mourning over the death of a loved one knows that the consolation of another is effective to the extent that the consoler is 1) someone we love and 2) someone who can be present to us and united with us in our time of grief. This presence and union with one we love is exactly what the word *consoled* in the Greek text implies. It is derived from the same word as *paraclete*, that is, comforter or advocate, and it is a compound of two words that together mean "called to one's side." An advocate is someone who is called to your side to help you.

And so, this consolation involves a union with someone we trust can help us. In Scripture, both the Son and the Holy Spirit are called "paraclete": the Son is called a paraclete in the first epistle of John (2:1) and the Holy Spirit is called "another paraclete" in John's Gospel (14:16, DRA). So the consolation promised in this second Beatitude implies a union with the Son and the Holy Spirit. If we are mourning over the death of Christ, we are rewarded by union with the risen Christ. If we are mourning over the death of our own soul, we are rewarded by union with the Holy Spirit, who is the life of our soul.

Those who hope in the goodness and power of God and believe what he has promised can also hope that their loved ones will be "called to their side" in the final resurrection. Even those who mourn by putting their bodies to death by penance are consoled by the hope that their bodies will be "called to the side" of their souls at the future reunion with their bodies in the resurrection to eternal life.

In short, just as mourning implies separation from those we love, so consolation implies a permanent and lasting reunion with those we love. Therefore, this consolation is the just and appropriate reward for those who mourn.

The example of Christ and the saints

In becoming man, the Son of God had no other aim than to redeem us by his passion and death. Having life within himself, and being free from sin and guilt, Jesus did not have to suffer and die. Yet that is just what he did: "He humbled himself, becoming obedient to death, even death on a cross" (Phil. 2:8, NAB). He fasted for forty days and nights, and when Satan tempted him to make bread for himself, he refused. During his passion, though he could have allowed the glory of the Beatific Vision to overflow into his body, as he did during the Transfiguration, he chose rather to prevent this so that he could suffer more readily.[33] And his suffering both bodily and emotionally exceeded all others'.[34] For having a perfectly tempered body,

THOSE WHO MOURN

he could feel pain most perfectly. Moreover, he was aware of his dignity and innocence, and so in his soul he suffered more than any other could suffer over the loss of his life. And, finally because of his great love for others, he suffered more than any other could suffer at the hardness and rejection of sinners.

The Blessed Virgin Mary also gave us an example of voluntary suffering, so much so that she is invoked as Our Lady of Sorrows. Like her son, she had no sin for which to atone, and so all her suffering was voluntary. Simeon foretold her sufferings with the prophetic word: "A sword will pierce through your own soul also" (Luke 2:35). Thus, St. Bernard said of her, "[Jesus] died in body through a love greater than anyone had known. She died in spirit through a love unlike any other since his."[35]

St. Rose of Lima

From her youth, Rose of Lima was accustomed to practicing severe penances. She did this not out of an exaggerated sense of guilt or self–loathing. On the contrary, she was well aware that God had preserved her baptismal innocence and that she was an object of special love. Yet she also understood that to be united in the saving mission of Christ, we must voluntarily make reparation for others. And so her penances were suffused with love for God and neighbor. She also saw how love for the things of this world extinguished love for heavenly realities. She so longed for the glory of heaven that she was willing to endure every sorrow. After hearing from Christ that the cross is the only true stairway to paradise, she cried out,

We cannot obtain grace unless we suffer afflictions. We must heap trouble upon trouble to obtain a deep participation in the divine nature, the glory of the sons of God

71

and perfect beatitude of soul . . . If only mortals would learn how great it is to possess divine grace, how beautiful, how noble, how precious. How many riches it hides within itself, how many joys and delights! Without doubt they would devote all their care and concern to winning for themselves pains and afflictions. All men throughout the world would seek infirmities and torments instead of good fortune in order to obtain the unfathomable treasure of grace. No one would complain about his cross or troubles that may happen to him, if he would come to know the scales on which they were weighed when they are distributed to men.[36]

This advice she gave to others, she lived exactly herself. And having been told the very day of her death, she willingly accepted in advance a most agonizing death, marked more by supernatural sufferings than natural ones. Even during her death agony of more than three weeks, which went beyond the limits of natural human endurance, she accepted over and over again the sufferings offered to her. All of this shows how she was moved by the gifts of the Holy Spirit to love that which human nature most naturally shuns in order to attain a joy beyond the capacity of human nature.

To which gift and petition of the Our Father does this Beatitude correspond?

It is difficult to correlate mourning with a gift of the Holy Spirit, since no gift seems to have mourning as its proper activity. For example, the proper activity of the gift of knowledge seems to be right judgment, and the proper activity of the gift of counsel seems to be to direct others to their good, and so on with the other gifts.

To understand how certain gifts correspond to certain Beatitudes, it is necessary to see that each Beatitude has a first part, which gives the reason for merit, and a second part that indicates the appropriate reward. And so, each Beatitude has an element pertaining to the active life, through which we merit, and an element pertaining to the contemplative life, in which we enjoy the reward of merit. For example, the activity of mourning rightly is meritorious, and being consoled is a reward of our meritorious mourning.

Therefore, when we seek to correlate "blessed are those who mourn" with a gift of the Holy Spirit, we are seeking how a gift produces some action that is meritorious (pertaining to the active life). It is precisely the gift of knowledge that results in a meritorious mourning. For when someone experiences the pleasant goods of this life, if he is virtuous he moderates his desires so as to use these pleasant things rightly. But by means of a gift of the Holy Spirit, not only does a man make reasonable use of such pleasant goods, but he also judges by the gift of knowledge their vanity and passing nature, as well as those times when they are an impediment to future glory. Consequently, he chooses even to spurn earthly pleasures and to mourn. Thus, St. Thomas writes:

> From following the concupiscible passions, man is withdrawn: by a virtue, so that man uses these passions in moderation; and by gift [of the Holy Spirit], so that, if necessary, he casts them aside altogether; nay more, so that, if need be, he makes a deliberate choice of sorrow. Hence the third Beatitude is: "Blessed are they that mourn."[37]

The connection between knowledge and mourning is made clear in the book of Ecclesiastes:

I applied my mind to seek and to search out by wisdom all that is done under heaven; it is an unhappy business that God has given to the sons of men to be busy with. I have seen everything that is done under the sun; and behold, all is vanity and a striving after wind. What is crooked cannot be made straight, and what is lacking cannot be numbered. I said to myself, "I have acquired great wisdom, surpassing all who were over Jerusalem before me; and my mind has had great experience of wisdom and knowledge." And I applied my mind to know wisdom and to know madness and folly. I perceived that this also is but a striving after wind. For in much wisdom is much vexation, and he who increases knowledge increases sorrow (1:13–18).

The knowledge and wisdom of "all that is done under heaven," that is, all created things, ultimately leads to sorrow. For there is no happiness to be found among all creatures. Only what is eternal and uncreated brings true happiness.

Overcoming difficulties in living out this Beatitude: the problem of suffering

In John's Gospel, Jesus gives his apostles some instruction on the second Beatitude:

Truly, truly, I say to you, you will weep and lament, but the world will rejoice; you will be sorrowful, but your sorrow will turn into joy. When a woman is in travail she has sorrow, because her hour has come; but when she is delivered of the child, she no longer remembers the anguish, for joy that a child is born into the world. So you have sorrow now, but I will see you again and your hearts will rejoice, and no one will take your joy from you (16:20–22).

Here Jesus offers a response to the problem of intense suffering. The first thing he tells them is that sorrow in this life is inescapable. He makes this clear by the use of the formula "Truly, truly" or "Amen, amen." These words signify that the next statement is completely certain. So it is completely certain, according to the word of Truth himself, that those who are not of the world will weep and lament.

One consequence of this fact is that we should not try to avoid or run away from sorrow. We will only be wasting time and energy. Sorrow will find us soon enough. So often people try to avoid suffering by forms of emotional anesthesia: alcohol, drugs, eating, spending hours on the internet or watching television, pornography; even shopping and gambling. None of these things will help us, and in fact they will add new crosses of our own making, crosses much heavier than the ones our loving Father has prepared for us.

The second thing Jesus teaches us is that "the world will rejoice." This is important to realize because the rejoicing of the world will make the life of mourning seem that much more difficult by contrast. The Psalmist points out this difficulty many times. One text from Psalm 73 is particularly poignant:

But, as for me, I lost my balance; my feet all but slipped, because I was envious of the arrogant when I saw the prosperity of the wicked. For they suffer no pain; their bodies are healthy and sleek. They are free of the burdens of life; they are not afflicted like others. Thus pride adorns them as a necklace; violence clothes them as a robe. Out of their stupidity comes sin; evil thoughts flood their hearts. They scoff and spout their malice; from on high they utter threats. They set their mouths against the heavens, their tongues roam the earth. So my people turn to them and drink deeply of their words. They say,

"Does God really know?" "Does the Most High have any knowledge?" Such, then, are the wicked, always carefree, increasing their wealth. Is it in vain that I have kept my heart clean, washed my hands in innocence? For I am afflicted day after day, chastised every morning (vv.2–14, NAB).

It is hard enough to go through suffering; it is even harder to do so when others around you are prospering, and harder still when their evil lives are the very reason for their prosperity. Jesus wants to prepare us for the inevitable fact that if our following the Gospel brings sacrifice and a certain amount of suffering, then those who do not follow the Gospel will not be subject to the same suffering. If speaking the truth about someone's wicked actions brings retaliation, staying silent will avoid retaliation, and approving may even bring rewards. Many bishops remained silent over the unlawful marriages of Henry VIII, for instance, and others even publicly supported it. These were promoted. But Sts. John Fisher and Thomas More would not acquiesce, and for that reason they met their death.

Another reason the rejoicing of the world can cause problems is that it makes us wonder if God is really in charge. Doubts like, "Does God really know?" and, "Does the Most High have any knowledge?" assail the heart of the just one who suffers while observing the prosperity of the wicked. Added to these doubts are others like them: "Does God really care?" and, "Is God really just?" The book of Job is a response to these doubts, which are all comprised by the question, "Why do bad things happen to good people, and good things happen to bad people?" The heart of the answer to this question is that there is another life after this one, and perfect justice will only be accomplished there.

The fact that the world will rejoice shows us that it is important not to be envious or to contrast our sorrows with the prosperity of others. This only saps our strength. If a soldier sits in his foxhole thinking about the lives of those who are sitting comfortably at home, he will lose his strength to fight. On the other hand, soldiers who, though suffering together in battle, do not waste time comparing their lives to the lives of others take strength from their mutual love and support, and their brotherhood is strengthened through shared suffering. So too, women who are surrounded by other women who, in spite of the accompanying burdens, rejoice in having many children, find the strength and courage to be generous in giving life. But if a woman surrounds herself with those who constantly complain about the difficulties of raising children, she will hardly find the strength to raise even the few children she has. The truth of our human experience is complaint and envy can turn a perfectly bearable sorrow into despair, whereas encouragement and mutual support can turn a nearly unbearable burden into something willingly borne.

The third lesson Jesus teaches us in this passage is that "our sorrow will be turned into joy." Notice, he does not say "replaced by joy" but rather "turned into joy" as if the sorrow itself will be the matter from which our joy will take its shape. I like to give a very simple example that illustrates this.

Let us say your favorite team is competing in the championship game. Victory can come in one of three forms: 1) your team is comfortably ahead the entire game and wins in a blowout; 2) the game is close the whole way, but your team manages to pull out a win at the end; or 3) your team is behind by a lot for most of the game, everything looks hopeless, but somehow, at the very end, your team makes a miraculous come-from-behind victory. Every sports fan who has experienced each of these scenarios knows that the first kind of victory is satisfying, the second more so, but the last is exhilarating. This is because the joy you feel at the end of the game is directly proportional to the sadness you felt while your team's chances looked hopeless.

God wants each of our lives to be a dramatic, even miraculous, come-from-behind victory so that we can experience the greatest degree of joy possible. This is why St. Peter writes that we should "rejoice in so far as you share Christ's sufferings, that you may also rejoice and be glad when his glory is revealed" (1 Pet. 4:13). And Paul says even more plainly: "For as we share abundantly in Christ's sufferings, so through Christ we share abundantly in comfort too. . . . for we know that as you share in our sufferings, you will also share in our comfort" (2 Cor. 1:5, 7). It was for this reason that saints such as Rose of Lima could say that if we only knew what great graces come through suffering, we would spend our lives seeking opportunities to suffer, heaping on ourselves trouble upon trouble.

The final lesson Jesus teaches us is that we must learn to *forget our suffering*: "When a woman is in travail she has sorrow, because her hour has come; but when she is delivered of the child, she no longer remembers the anguish, for joy that a child is born into the world." Studies show that women produce chemicals that cause them to forget some of the pain they experienced in childbirth. And there are certain kinds of anesthesia that function primarily by preventing us from forming memories of the pain we experience. In fact, the remembrance of past sufferings can be a great obstacle to the spiritual life and to further spiritual growth.

Even a soul as great as St. Paul struggled with this. On one occasion, Jesus visited Paul to console him and assure him that the pain of past failures would not repeat themselves: "One night in a vision the Lord said to Paul, 'Do not be afraid. Go on speaking, and do not be silent, for I am with you. No one will attack and harm you, for I have many people in this city'" (Acts 18:9–10, NAB). We need to do the same thing as Paul: forget past sufferings and move forward in doing good. Jesus always encourages us to live in the moment. The past cannot be changed and the future does not yet exist. The only time in which we can do good is now.

At each moment of our lives there is a grace and a joy that God wants to give us, but the devil tries to convince us to live in the past and the future, and by so doing to prevent us from receiving that joy and grace. And since only the present moment is real, if the devil can convince us to live in the past or some imagined future, he will prevent us from doing any good. By remembering past suffering, we tend to project it into the future, which paralyzes us in the present.

If we succeed in focusing upon the present, and we find suffering in that present moment, how can we act so as to continue making progress through that suffering? In my own experience, I have noticed that even the pain of the present moment can be magnified or diminished depending upon the object of our attention. For example, while playing an intense sport like football or rugby, I have noticed that after the game there are all sorts of wounds and bruises that I didn't even remember getting during the game because I was so focused upon the game itself. If I had been quietly meditating upon myself and someone did those things to me, I would have felt those wounds and bruises in all their excruciating detail. Yet because I was intensely focused upon something other than myself, I barely noticed those same wounds and bruises.

The spiritual life is much the same. If we are focused primarily upon ourselves, we will feel every slight, every rejection, every physical and spiritual wound. But if we are intensely focused upon loving and living for others, we will often not even notice the sufferings that come with following Christ faithfully in this life.

Of course, the primary person to love and live for is Jesus Christ. If we focus upon him and remember the sufferings that he and his blessed mother endured for our sake, our ability to endure suffering, even joyfully accept it, will be greatly enhanced. And then we shall already, in this life, begin to experience the truth of the Beatitude. Blessed are those who mourn, for they shall be consoled.

THE MEEK

It is better to be of a lowly spirit with the poor than to
divide the spoil with the proud (Prov. 16:19).

After pronouncing those who mourn to be blessed, the Lord directs his praises to the meek: "Blessed are the meek, for they shall inherit the land." Whereas the Beatitude about mourning concerned the dispositions of the sense appetite that desires pleasure, this Beatitude concerns the dispositions of the sense appetite that strives to overcome obstacles to pleasure. *Anger* is the emotion that most noticeably motivates us to overcome difficulties and obstacles, and so the irascible appetite is named from this emotion (*ira* is the Latin word for anger, from which we also get the English word *ire*).

That firm disposition of soul that moderates anger reasonably is called *meekness*, so the Lord teaches that it is this disposition, and its corresponding act, that merits the reward of inheriting the land.

Who are the meek?

Meekness is a virtue that tempers our tendency to excessive or unreasonable anger. The actions proceeding from meekness are, therefore, gentle. Now, anger itself is not evil. It is possible to be meek and to be angry, as the Lord himself showed when he drove out the moneychangers in the temple.[38] But it is not possible to be meek and to be *unreasonably* angry. Thus, the meek are characterized by gentleness and patience in the face of evil and injustice.

Yet far from being doormats, the meek are firm in their resolution to do good and love others rightly. They do not cower in fear but remain strong in their silence before injustice and, if necessary, respond forcefully to evil by fraternal correction. The Lord Jesus gave us an extraordinary example of this meekness before Pilate and Herod: "As a sheep led to the slaughter or a lamb before its shearer is dumb, so he opens not his mouth" (Acts 8:32).

In a broader sense, meekness can also be taken to signify humility and those other virtues that moderate the desire to dominate others. The Lord commends such virtues when he teaches his disciples:

> Jesus summoned them and said to them: "You know that those who are recognized as rulers over the Gentiles lord it over them, and their great ones make their authority over them felt. But it shall not be so among you. Rather, whoever wishes to be great among you will be your servant" (Mark 10:42–43, NAB).

Just as the poor in spirit are interiorly detached from wealth, so are the meek interiorly detached from *power* and its use. And those who are motivated by the gifts of the Holy Spirit positively spurn any show of power or authority over others.

Why is the reward "they will inherit the land" appropriate?

The reward promised by this Beatitude seems to be completely inappropriate. For the word *land* or *earth* (both possible translations of the Greek term *gen*) seems to signify something base and ignoble. After all, the earth seems to be opposed to heaven, so this reward seems to exclude any heavenly reward.

In fact, Scripture also applies these words to heavenly realities. For example, in the Psalms we read, "I shall walk before the Lord in the land of the living" (116:9, NAB), and again: "But I believe I shall enjoy the Lord's goodness in the land of the living" (27:13, NAB). Here the sense of *land* is a firm and stable possession rather than something base and ignoble. Thus, the reward "they shall inherit the land" means their heavenly Father will give them the land of heaven forever.

A second reason why the reward promised in this Beatitude seems less appropriate is that the reward for the meek seems like it ought to be something like power or authority, since the meek are those who do not lord it over others or seek to dominate others. Thus, it seems that a more appropriate reward would be "they will exercise great authority" or something like that.

But consider this question: Why are power and authority desirable? Are these things good in themselves or are they good for something else? Many people have power but are very unhappy. In reality, power and authority are good only because they allow us to firmly possess some other good that makes us truly happy. Someone who is powerful can keep the goods he has and no one else can take them from him. Thus, Jesus said, "When a strong man, fully armed, guards his own palace, his goods are in peace" (Luke 11:21).

So, power is only good to the extent that it allows us to firmly possess something truly good. Therefore, a better reward than power, and a more fitting one for the blessed who eschew power, is the very thing that power is supposed to guarantee: the firm and stable possession of heavenly goods.

Pope St. Leo the Great understands the *land* here to refer to the resurrected bodies of the saints:

> To the meek and gentle, the humble and modest, and to those who are prepared to endure all injuries, the earth is promised as their possession. And this is not to be reckoned a small or cheap inheritance, as if it were distinct from our heavenly dwelling, since it is no other than these who are understood to enter the kingdom of heaven. The earth, then, which is promised to the meek, and is to be given to the gentle in possession, is the flesh of the saints which in reward for their humility will be changed in a happy resurrection, and clothed with the glory of immortality, in nothing now to act contrary to the spirit, and to be in complete unity and agreement with the will of the soul. For then the outer man will be the peaceful and unblemished possession of the inner man.[39]

In this sense also, the reward is appropriate. For it is appropriate that one who trained and moderated his bodily passions when they resisted his reason should receive as a reward a body completely docile to his reason.

Overcoming difficulties in living out this Beatitude

Meekness is not weakness, but we tend to identify these two things. And we are afraid of weakness. Someone who is weak is uncertain if he will continue to possess the goods that he thinks are necessary for happiness. From this uncertainty and fear arises the desire for power and domination over others. We are afraid of losing our property, our health, our friendships, and other important relationships. And we think that by means of power we can secure all these goods so we will never lose them. As a result, in our hearts we think, *Cursed are the meek, for they shall lose every good thing.*

Before addressing the root of the problem, let us first consider whether or not power will accomplish what it seems to promise. Will power keep us from losing our property? For example, will being able to win a fight or owning a lot of guns keep our wallet or home safe? Perhaps for a time. But there will always be someone who is more powerful. And our very power might make us a target of those who are more powerful than we—for the powerful are not envious of the weak, but of those who are their rivals. And even if we are able to fend off the attacks of others, will we ultimately be able to fend off death? So, power as a means of maintaining property is at best only a temporary help.

Will power infallibly allow us to maintain our health, which is much more valuable than our property? Here power is even more likely to fail. Even if we could find and pay the best doctors in the world, the limits of medical knowledge and art, as well as the limits of our fallen human nature, make health a very precarious thing. There are many very wealthy and powerful people who can do nothing about their health. Scripture tells us of a woman of great substance who had wasted her money on doctors for twelve years, but still could not stop her hemorrhage (Luke 8:43). And even if the power of doctors can be employed to prolong our life, how much of that life will be spent in suffering and illness? Power guarantees little or nothing with regard to health.

Finally, can power be used to guarantee that we will maintain our friendships and most cherished relationships? Here it is most obvious that power fails. One thing that can never be obtained or possessed by force is love. By its nature, love is a free response. Force may be able to elicit fear, but never love. Power is never more powerless than in its attempts to secure love.

So the limitations of power are apparent, even to those who have no faith. But in spite of these limitations, many continue to pursue power and to try to secure goods by force. In order to put a stop to this false pursuit, the Lord proclaimed, "Blessed are the meek."

The root of the problem for those who find it difficult to live out this Beatitude is *fear*. Their fear makes them weak instead of meek. In order to be meek, we need to trust; just as a small child is without fear when being protected by his father, so too the meek live without fear. Therefore, the key disposition necessary to live out this Beatitude is *trust* in divine providence. The meek are self-controlled because they do not think they must control everything else. Their trust in God's providence allows them to let go of the need to control their environment and relationships. Convinced of their Father's loving care and all-reaching governance of the world, they are secure in how things are being governed by the Lord, and see no need to improve upon his designs. They trust that "all things work for good for those who love God, who are called according to his purpose" (Rom. 8:28, NAB).

Their meekness, rooted in trust of divine goodness, makes it possible for them to hold firmly the goods that power could never secure. Chief among these is God himself and eternal life with him. The meek man holds property, health, and friendships dear only to the extent that these contribute to eternal life. And he is confident that God shall dispose these created goods in the manner most conducive to inheriting eternal life.

So, where the weak are fearful and unstable in their dispositions, the meek are courageous and firm. There is nothing as strong as a meek man, for his strength is the Lord's own strength.

The example of Christ and the saints

Jesus offers the faithful a perfect example of how to live this Beatitude. He told us that we must learn meekness from him, for he is "meek and humble of heart" (Matt. 11:29). He did not come as a great ruler or military leader, and his birth was mean and humble. Divine power was made incarnate in obscurity and lowliness, like the small whispering sound that the prophet Elijah heard on Mount Horeb (1 Kings 19:12). One who is truly powerful need not make a show to impress others.

As man, Jesus lived most of his life in obscurity, and when he began his public ministry, he refused to be made a powerful king either by the devil or by the crowds (Matt. 4:8–10; Luke 4:5–8; John 6:15). He performed miracles only to strengthen the faith of others, not for his own glory or even to save his own life. When he was struck in the face by the Jewish guards and on the head by the Roman soldiers, he remained silent and did not get angry: "When he was insulted, he returned no insult; when he suffered, he did not threaten; instead, he handed himself over to the one who judges justly" (1 Pet. 2:23, NAB). Finally, though he had the power to command twelve legions of angels, instead he allowed himself to be arrested, unjustly tried, and put to death.

As God, Jesus showed the greatest meekness possible, "taking the form of a servant" (Phil. 2:7) and humbling himself unto death. There is a special reason why the second Person of the Trinity should manifest in his divine nature the perfection corresponding to meekness. For, as Son,

Christ received his whole being from the Father by way of an eternal procession. Thus, it is especially appropriate that the perfection of meekness that acknowledges all that we have and are as a gift, be manifested in God the Son.

Moses

The scriptures assert that Moses was "by far the meekest man on the face of the earth" (Num. 12:3, NAB). This praise is even more admirable considering that as a young man he was so easily stirred to anger that he killed an Egyptian in his wrath! But as he grew in virtue and confidence in the Lord's mercy, he became exceedingly meek. On many occasions, the Israelites grumbled against Moses, constantly attributing evil motives to him, yet he was not bitter and he did not threaten them with God's punishment. Instead, Moses would prostrate himself on the ground and beg them to obey the Lord. Even when Miriam and Aaron spoke against Moses because of their jealousy, and God in his anger made Miriam a leper, Moses begged God to heal Miriam.

It is particularly interesting that Moses is identified as the meekest man on earth, yet he did not inherit the Promised Land. God would not allow him to enter. Perhaps this was to show that Moses would inherit a better land, the land of the living.

To which gift and petition of the Our Father does this Beatitude correspond?

The worldly believe that happiness consists in following your passions. And one of the principal passions is anger. Anger always results from a perceived injustice. Today in the world we find so many people striving to dominate others, so many loud and violent protests and movements, because they believe that the only way to be happy is to follow where their anger leads.

In contrast, the virtue of meekness inclines us to moderate our anger so that our actions are reasonable; so that we rightly weigh the injustice and respond appropriately. In an even more excellent way, the gift of *piety* causes us to completely trust in divine providence so that we submit ourselves completely to the divine governance and rests secure. For by piety we render due honor and respect to those above us: our parents, our country, and especially God. Even if someone is subject to an extreme injustice from a temporal perspective, if he is pious he submits to divine government; he believes that God is a just judge who orders all things rightly. He says with blessed Job, "The Lord gave, and the Lord has taken away; blessed be the name of the Lord" (Job 1:21). For this reason, the Beatitude "blessed are the meek" corresponds to the gift of piety.

From this it is also clear that this Beatitude corresponds to the petition "thy kingdom come," since one who submits himself to divine government ardently longs for its coming. Thus, St. Thomas writes:

> Through this petition we arrive at the Beatitude "blessed are the meek." For according to the first explanation, namely, that a man desires that God be the Lord over all things, he does not vindicate himself concerning injuries against him, but he leaves that to God. For if you vindicate yourself, you do not seek the coming of his kingdom.[40]

The certain hope that God's kingdom will come causes those who practice gentleness and meekness through the gift of piety to rest secure already in the land of the living.

6

THOSE WHO HUNGER AND THIRST FOR RIGHTEOUSNESS

Those who eat me will hunger for more, and those who
drink me will thirst for more (Sir. 24:21).

After blessing the meek, the Lord goes on to proclaim that those who *hunger and thirst for righteousness* are also blessed. This begins the next set of Beatitudes, in which the reason for merit pertains now to the common good of our neighbor: namely, that righteousness and justice may be established among men.

Who are those who hunger and thirst for righteousness?

In one sense, this Beatitude applies to those who desire justice. All men desire what is just toward *them*. Small children will immediately object if their sibling is given a larger piece of cake or scoop of ice cream than they receive. And even the most obstinate moral relativist immediately becomes a card-carrying moral objectivist when someone steals from him, or physically harms him, or commits some other injustice toward him. And so, the desire for justice toward us is natural, easy even for children and the badly formed to see.

What is not so clear to most people is that justice should also be shown to *others*. Even if most people admit that we should do unto others as we would have them do unto us, when it comes to particular instances most people have a hard time empathizing with their neighbor. It is therefore the product of virtue when someone desires what is truly just for others. And when someone, moved by the gifts of the Holy Spirit, not only desires but so ardently desires justice for his neighbors that it is described as hunger and thirst, this Beatitude applies most truly.

In a broader sense, the Greek word used in this Beatitude, *dikaiosune* (translated here as "righteousness"), can be understood to mean uprightness in the sense of one having all the virtues. When it is understood in this way, those who hunger and thirst for uprightness are those who long for every virtue to be established among men. But since the Beatitudes proceed not just from virtue but from the gifts of the Holy Spirit, righteousness or uprightness should principally be understood to refer to rectitude in the sight of God through the three theological virtues: faith, hope, and especially charity. Thus, those who hunger and thirst for righteousness ardently long for the *establishment of the right relationship between God and men.*

A word should be said about the use of the metaphors *hunger* and *thirst* in this Beatitude. Jesus could have just said "desire greatly," but instead he chose to say "hunger and thirst." One reason for this to impress upon even those who are simple the intensity and concreteness of this desire. Everyone, whatever his degree of spiritual maturity, understands just how strong hunger and thirst are. And hunger and thirst clearly move us to action. So too, our hunger and thirst for righteousness is a *principle of action* to establish this righteousness in our own souls and in the souls of others. It is this action, not just the desire, that is meritorious and causes blessedness.

Another reason for using this language is the fact that hunger and thirst are natural desires. In order for human nature to be complete, food and drink must be obtained. So also the desire for virtue is natural, and human nature cannot be complete without it. Righteousness is necessary for human fulfillment—not merely optional or an accessory.

Another reason why the Lord may have said "hunger and thirst" is that we find food pleasant and delightful. So too, then, we ought to find righteousness and virtue delightful.

Hunger and thirst also imply a recurring or continual desire, as if to say that no matter how much righteousness you experience, you will still want more: "Those who eat me will hunger for more, and those who drink me will thirst for more" (Sir. 24:21).

Last of all, hunger and thirst call to mind the Eucharist, our spiritual food. St. Paul calls Jesus "our righteousness" (1 Cor. 1:30). Therefore, those who hunger and thirst for righteousness are those who hunger and thirst for Christ in the Eucharist.

Why in Luke does Jesus simply say, "Blessed are you who hunger and thirst"?

Just as Luke had only "blessed are you poor," so here we read simply "blessed are you who hunger and thirst." Is Luke asserting that Jesus taught that it is enough for someone to be physically hungry or thirsty for them to be blessed?

Jesus himself rejects this view when he tells the crowds, "Do not labor for the food which perishes, but for the food which endures to eternal life, which the Son of man will give to you" (John 6:27). Jesus is not praising them for seeking bodily food, but rather spiritual food, and especially the Eucharist.

So how do we understand Luke's statement? Here again we must remember the context of this sermon. Crowds of people have come to follow Jesus from far off. They have been with him for a long time and many have run out of food. This implies that these crowds long to hear the teaching of Jesus more than to eat or drink! So, Jesus addresses them directly: the people right in front of him who have forsaken bodily food to live by every word that proceeds from the mouth of God. He says, "Blessed are you," not "Blessed are those." Their physical hunger and thirst are signs of an even deeper spiritual hunger and thirst for righteousness. Pope St. Leo the Great teaches:

> It is nothing bodily, nothing earthly, that this hunger, this thirst seeks for: but it desires to be satiated with the good food of righteousness, and wants to be admitted to all the deepest mysteries, and be filled with the Lord himself. Happy the mind that craves this food and is eager for such drink, which it certainly would not seek for if it had never tasted of its sweetness. But hearing the prophet's spirit saying to him, "Taste and see that the Lord is sweet," it has received some portion of sweetness from on high.[41]

Luke probably does not add "for righteousness" because he was reporting the exact words of the Lord. And the Lord wanted to reassure the crowds in front of him that the fact that they were poor and without food did not exclude them from blessedness. On the contrary, because their hunger and thirst were voluntarily chosen in order to follow him, it was a sign of God's favor. Moreover, those who are hungry and thirsty are more able to be compassionate with others who are hungry and thirsty. Mother Teresa used to say that in order to understand the poor we must experience poverty and in order to understand the hungry we must experience hunger. So, in this way even those who suffer actual physical hunger and thirst are blessed. And in this way also the Lord commends fasting and abstinence.

What is the reward promised and why is it appropriate?

The reward promised to those who hunger and thirst for righteousness is that they shall "have their fill," or "be satisfied." It is obvious why the appropriate reward for those who hunger and thirst is to have that hunger and thirst satisfied. And they shall be satisfied or filled with righteousness, not just physical food; experiencing not only moral rectitude in themselves but living in the company of saints. Thus, they shall live in a perfectly just society. And their satisfaction will not extend only to the satisfaction of their desire for moral rectitude; they shall have *every* desire of the human heart satisfied by the vision of God. In this way, the reward exceeds the cause for merit, since God gives even more than we can desire or work for.

In a sense, this reward also pertains to the present life. Jesus said, "Seek first the kingdom of God and his righteousness, and all these things will be given you besides" (Matt. 6:33, NAB). Thus, God will satisfy our natural desires even for things of this world insofar as these things are necessary or useful for attaining the righteousness we desire.

The Greek word *chortasthesontai*, translated here as "will be satisfied," originally refers to feeding or fattening cattle in a stall. This implies that they shall not have to work to acquire this food in the life to come, but God himself will provide this spiritual food and drink for their souls, while they stand and rest in his presence. And all of this is just and appropriate for those who have desired righteousness above all else and who have worked to achieve it.

How can we overcome difficulties in living out this Beatitude?

The great obstacle to living out this Beatitude is that we tend to know and appreciate lesser goods better than we know and appreciate greater goods. So rather than hungering and thirsting for righteousness, we hunger and thirst for material things. And rather than hungering and thirsting that justice be established for all, we hunger and thirst for what is due to us. This self-centered love of the least goods, which is the starting point for those born in original sin, mightily opposes the hunger and thirst for righteousness.

The first thing that needs to happen is our eyes must be opened to the real order of goods; that is, we must learn to see that spiritual goods are greater than material goods. Part of this learning process comes from experience, and part from trust in those who already see for themselves.

Experience teaches us that material goods inevitably disappoint us. We may eat and drink as much as we like, but three things usually happen if we indulge our desires for physical food and drink: we feel bloated and slow, and then in a short time we feel hungry all over again, and after all that we become obese from overeating. And this kind of thing happens not only with food, but with any good that satisfies only our emotions. If we try to find emotional satisfaction in a human relationship, seeking to be and feel loved, we are inevitably disappointed. Passing goods promise much but deliver little. This is why St. John says simply, "The world is passing away along with its desires" (1 John 2:17, ESV). So experience teaches us to value material, passing goods less and less.

Sometimes God intervenes in our lives to starkly manifest to us the insufficiency of created and material goods. A young woman is infatuated with a man who suddenly dies in a tragic accident. A young man has dreams of making great wealth on a business deal, then he is cheated out of everything he owns. A married couple are obsessed with living a life of luxury, when suddenly their child gets cancer. Experiences like these have a way of recalibrating our lives.

On the other hand, trust in those who already see the right order of goods for themselves helps us to value spiritual goods more. Even someone with very little virtue can usually identify a virtuous person. It is not hard to see that Mother Teresa of Calcutta or Padre Pio is virtuous. These people have already traversed the order of goods, and they see clearly from experience that spiritual goods infinitely excel material goods. And even among spiritual goods, they can say which are greater. If we are willing to trust someone virtuous as a guide for our spiritual life to seek after certain spiritual goods more and to follow the path he sets out for us, we will find those goods and begin to experience for ourselves the joys they bring. Gradually, in this way, we begin to perceive the true order of goods, and things like ice cream (or their adult equivalents) will attract us less and less while things like prayer and justice will attract us more and more.

A second thing that needs to happen if we are to overcome difficulties in living this Beatitude: we need to *grow in empathy* so that we see others as we see ourselves. Although it may be helpful to experience the sufferings that others experience—their poverty, their hunger, their shame—just experiencing these things is not enough. Suffering can make a soul turn inward as much as outward. Empathy means more than going through what another is going through, it also means identifying with the other. Empathy is the ability to *live within* another person. And this ability, although it has a natural dimension, is only fully realized in the supernatural order. Empathy first requires that we live in Christ, and then through Christ to live within the Christ who is in our neighbor. Paul describes this reality by means of the metaphor of the Mystical Body:

> Be renewed in the spirit of your minds, and put on the new self, created in God's way in righteousness and holiness of truth. Therefore, putting away falsehood, speak the truth, each one to his neighbor, for we are members one of another (Eph. 4:23–25, NAB).

First, he speaks about putting on the "new self," that is, Christ. Then he concludes that "we are members, one of another" since we all belong to that new self who is Christ. The most powerful way to do this is through the devout and frequent reception of Holy Communion, where our bodies are transformed spiritually into the body of Christ.

The example of Christ and the saints

Jesus gives to us the supreme example of hungering and thirsting for righteousness. From the cross he cried out, "I thirst!" In the desert, he fasted for forty days and was hungry. And when he sat down at the well in Samaria, he both hungered and thirsted for the faith and love of the Samaritan people. In all these texts, it was much more than a bodily hunger and thirst that the Lord experienced. Rather he was hungering and thirsting that a right relationship be restored between God and man. Proof of that comes when the disciples tried to get Jesus to eat after he spoke with the Samaritan woman at the well:

> Meanwhile the disciples besought him, saying, "Rabbi, eat." But he said to them: "I have food to eat of which you do not know." So the disciples said to one another, "Has any one brought him food?" Jesus said to them, "My food is to do the will of him who sent me, and to accomplish his work" (John 4:31–34).

Jesus had been physically hungry: that's why the disciples went to buy food. But his physical hunger was a sign, one might even say a sacrament, of his spiritual hunger. It was this spiritual hunger and thirst that moved him to bring about the conversion of the Samaritan woman and her countrymen. This hunger and thirst came to its culmination on the cross, when Jesus said, "I thirst." St. Teresa of Calcutta explains the significance of these words of Jesus:

> At this most difficult time he proclaimed, "I thirst." And people thought he was thirsty in an ordinary way and they gave him vinegar straight away; but it was not for that thirst; it was for our love, our affection, that intimate attachment to him, and that sharing of his passion. He used, "I thirst," instead of, "Give me your love" . . . "I thirst." Let us hear him saying it to me and saying it to you.[42]

St. Teresa of Calcutta

St. Teresa of Calcutta, better known simply as Mother Teresa, was a saint who lived out this Beatitude in a striking way. So intense was her own desire to live out this Beatitude that she made the words of Jesus, "I thirst," the theme of her entire spiritual life.

St. Teresa witnessed the grave injustices to which the poorest of the poor were subject, especially in India. She did not wait to form an organization to help the poor, she found a single person who needed her help and began there. And then she helped another and another. Her clients were the most abject of dying persons: lepers, people abandoned in garbage heaps and dung hills. Her aim was not so much to heal them all; most were beyond medical help. Rather, she desired to love them and make them feel loved by God. Her empathy for the poor defied natural explanation. Her hunger and thirst for justice was more profoundly a hunger and thirst for Christ. It was *Jesus* she saw in the distressing disguise of the poorest of the poor; it was righteousness himself for whom she thirsted. She famously said that she would never care for a leper even for a thousand pounds, but she would care for one out of love for Jesus.

These sentiments of her heart are expressed in a prayer she composed:

O God, we pray for all those in our world who are suffering from injustice: for those who are discriminated against because of their race, color, or religion; for those imprisoned for working for the relief of oppression; for those who are hounded for speaking the inconvenient truth; for those tempted to violence as a cry against overwhelming hardship; for those deprived of reasonable health and education; for those suffering from hunger and famine; for those too weak to help themselves and who have no one else to help them; for the unemployed who cry out for work but do not find it. We pray for anyone of our acquaintance who is personally affected by injustice. Forgive us, Lord, if we unwittingly share in the conditions or in a system that perpetuates injustice. Show us how we can serve your children and make your love practical by washing their feet.[43]

To which gift and petition of the Our Father does this Beatitude correspond?

Those who hunger and thirst are often tempted to give up for lack of strength. This is why the angel says to Elijah the prophet, "Arise and eat, else the journey will be too great for you" (1 Kings 19:7). After he ate and drank, the story continues: "He went in the strength of that food forty days and forty nights to Horeb the mount of God." Therefore, *fortitude* is the gift of the Holy Spirit that corresponds to this Beatitude. Fortitude allows us to persevere, not to faint from fear, in confronting injustice and believing firmly in all that Christ has taught. Thus, the prophet Isaiah says, "He gives power to the faint, and to him who has no might he increases strength. Even youths shall faint and be weary, and young men shall fall exhausted; but they who wait for the Lord shall renew their strength" (Isa. 40:29–31).

And it is fairly obvious that this Beatitude corresponds to the petition "give us this day our daily bread." For in this petition we ask not only for physical bread for our bodies, but also all the necessities of life, physical and spiritual. And most of all, we ask for the Eucharist, which is righteousness itself.

7

THE MERCIFUL

He will make room for every act of mercy; everyone will
receive in accordance with his deeds (Sir. 16:14).

Once justice and righteousness have been established among
men, it is possible to lead them to the even-greater perfection of mercy. For mercy goes beyond justice. The just
man takes no more than his fair share of goods, whereas the
merciful man accepts even *less* than what he is due, out of
love and compassion of his neighbor. Therefore, the Lord
proclaims the next Beatitude: "Blessed are the merciful, for
they will obtain mercy."

Who are the merciful?

Mercy is a particular form of goodness shown to others.
Sometimes we are good to others by being fair to them. This
is not mercy, but justice. Sometimes we are good to others by
showing them love and affection. This is not mercy, either,

but friendship. But when we are good to others by compassionately understanding the evils to which they are subject, and by taking away their miseries, this is mercy. So, the merciful are those who notice the evils that others suffer, have compassion upon them, and then act to remove those evils. These evils might be poverty, sickness, sadness, or even sin.

Of course, there is such a thing as false mercy. If someone were to recommend an abortion to alleviate the fear of a pregnant woman, or counsel divorce and remarriage to alleviate the sadness of a difficult marriage, these would not truly be instances of mercy. For they would involve the recipient in an even greater evil (sin) than that from which they were freed (physical and emotional suffering). Thus, true mercy requires a right understanding of what is truly good and truly evil.

Even those without faith can appreciate the goodness of being merciful. But the mercy of the Beatitude goes beyond what reason unaided by faith can appreciate. First, because the merciful of this Beatitude have a longing to dispel the misery of others even to the point of *accepting this misery upon themselves*. Furthermore, their mercy extends not only to friends and family but to *strangers and enemies*. Jesus describes this kind of mercy when he teaches his disciples, "When you give a dinner or a banquet, do not invite your friends or your brothers or your kinsmen or rich neighbors, lest they also invite you in return, and you be repaid. But when you give a feast, invite the poor, the maimed, the lame, the blind" (Luke 14:12–13).

Last of all, unlike those who appreciate the goodness of mercy at the natural level, the merciful of this Beatitude are motivated entirely by the *desire to help others attain the vision of God*, not some merely natural good. Pope St. Leo the Great emphasizes this supernatural motivation: "Mercy wishes you to be merciful, righteousness to be righteous, that the

Creator may be seen in his creature, and the image of God may be reflected in the mirror of the human heart expressed by the lines of imitation."[44]

What is their reward and how is it appropriate?

To the merciful, the reward promised is that they shall be shown mercy. The appropriateness of this reward is obvious, for it is intuitive that the way we have treated others should somehow determine the way we ourselves are treated. This is the foundation of the Golden Rule: "Do unto others as you would have them do unto you." Jesus teaches this on many occasions, such as after the Our Father, when he tells his disciples that they will be forgiven only on the condition that they forgive others (Matt. 6:14). He explains this teaching in greater detail through a parable:

> The kingdom of heaven may be compared to a king who wished to settle accounts with his servants. When he began the reckoning, one was brought to him who owed him ten thousand talents; and as he could not pay, his lord ordered him to be sold, with his wife and children and all that he had, and payment to be made. So the servant fell on his knees, imploring him, "Lord, have patience with me, and I will pay you everything." And out of pity for him the lord of that servant released him and forgave him the debt. But that same servant, as he went out, came upon one of his fellow servants who owed him a hundred denarii; and seizing him by the throat he said: "Pay what you owe." So his fellow servant fell down and besought him: "Have patience with me, and I will pay you." He refused and went and put him in prison till he should pay the debt. When his fellow servants saw what had taken

place, they were greatly distressed, and they went and reported to their lord all that had taken place. Then his lord summoned him and said to him: "You wicked servant! I forgave you all that debt because you besought me; and should not you have had mercy on your fellow servant, as I had mercy on you?" And in anger his lord delivered him to the jailers, till he should pay all his debt. So also my heavenly Father will do to every one of you, if you do not forgive your brother from your heart" (Matt. 18:23–35).

There is an obvious injustice in showing mercy to one who has not shown mercy. This is all the more true because the debt we owe is so much greater than the debt we are owed. Conversely, there is an obvious justice in showing mercy to one who has shown mercy. Thus, it is appropriate that God show mercy to those who have been merciful to their neighbors.

There is another reason for the appropriateness of this reward. It sometimes happens that a person suffers from his own problems, and so he is afraid to be merciful to others for fear that he will not have the resources to deal with his own miseries. For example, a man who is poor may be unwilling to give money to a beggar. But in order to remove this fear, God promises to come to the aid of those who show mercy to others. Thus, Thomas Aquinas says, "Some, recede from works of mercy, lest they be busied with other people's misery. Hence our Lord promised the merciful that they should obtain mercy, and be delivered from all misery."[45] So it is fitting that one who trusts in God to care for him should receive God's help.

What are the corporal and spiritual works of mercy?

Because man is composed of body and soul, there are works of mercy by which bodily miseries are remedied and works of mercy by which spiritual miseries are remedied. Christian tradition identifies seven corporal (bodily) and seven spiritual works of mercy:

Corporal Works of Mercy

1) Feed the hungry

2) Give drink to the thirsty

3) Clothe the naked

4) Shelter the homeless

5) Assist the sick

6) Visit the imprisoned/ransom captives

7) Bury the dead

Spiritual Works of Mercy

1) Instruct the ignorant

2) Counsel the doubtful

3) Comfort the sorrowing

4) Correct the sinner

5) Forgive offenses

6) Patiently bear another's burdens

7) Pray for the living and the dead

Because the soul is more important than the body, it is more important to remove spiritual miseries such as sin and error than to remove bodily miseries such as sickness and hunger. Therefore, the spiritual works of mercy are more important than the corporal works of mercy. Accordingly, when Jesus saw the great crowds, he first taught them to remove their ignorance, and then he fed them to remove their hunger:

> As he landed he saw a great throng, and he had compassion on them, because they were like sheep without a shepherd; and he began to teach them many things. And when it grew late, his disciples came to him and said, "This is a lonely place, and the hour is now late; send them away, to go into the country and villages round about and buy themselves something to eat." But he answered them, "You give them something to eat" (Mark 6:34–37).

Nevertheless, sometimes bodily needs are more urgent or necessary. Moreover, bodily needs are better known than spiritual needs. Therefore, it is sometimes more necessary to begin with corporal works of mercy, both to alleviate the more urgent miseries and to convince the spiritually immature that you care for their happiness in order to dispose them to accept spiritual help.

St. Thomas gives a reason why there are seven corporal and seven spiritual works of mercy.[46] As far as the needs of the body are concerned, some occur during life and others after death. During life, there are needs common to all men, such as food and drink, that are interior needs of man's body. From these needs the first two works of mercy arise: feeding the hungry and giving drink to the thirsty. There are also needs that are exterior, such as clothing and shelter, from which arise the third and fourth works of mercy: clothing the naked and sheltering the homeless. There are also needs peculiar to some men, and some of these are interior, like sickness, and others exterior, like imprisonment. From these needs the fifth and sixth works of mercy arise: assisting the sick and visiting or ransoming those in prison. Finally, there are the needs after death, and this need is addressed by the seventh work of mercy: the reverent burial of the dead, in which honor is displayed to the deceased and hope in a future resurrection.

St. Thomas gives a similar explanation for the spiritual works of mercy. There are some needs of the soul that can be addressed by asking help from other men, whereas others require that we ask God's help. Other men can supply the needs of the soul regarding defects in speculative or practical *knowledge*, and from these needs the first and second spiritual works of mercy arise: instructing the ignorant and counseling the doubtful. There is also a defect in the soul pertaining to our *desires*, namely, sadness. And from this need the third spiritual work of mercy arises: comforting the sorrowful. Finally, there are three defects in human *action* for which we can obtain human help: sin in another, sin in ourselves, and the effects of sin. From these three defects, the fourth, fifth, and sixth spiritual works of mercy arise: correcting the sinner, forgiving offenses, and patiently bearing one another's burdens. Last of all, there is the defect of soul that can only be remedied by asking God's assistance: alleviating the punishment due to sin in our souls, for which reason we pray for the dead and the living, which is the seventh spiritual work of mercy.

All of these corporal and spiritual works of mercy are ways of fulfilling the reason for merit in the fifth Beatitude, and thus being counted among the merciful who shall receive mercy.

The example of Christ and the saints

Jesus Christ was mercy incarnate, and in his every word and deed he showed the highest mercy toward men. As man,

Christ's entire life was spent removing the misery of others. He fed the hungry and instructed the ignorant, he healed the sick, he drove out demons, he forgave sins. On the cross, he forgave his murderers. As God, Jesus manifested mercy itself by becoming man and taking on our human nature.

The parable of the Good Samaritan is a parable about Jesus, who came to the aid of sinful humanity by pouring the wine of divine justice and the oil of divine mercy upon our wounds. Moreover, he lifted us upon his own beast, that is, his human nature, and brought us to an inn; that is, he provided a Church for our physical and spiritual care until he comes again. Jesus truly became our neighbor by showing us mercy.

St. Faustina

Among the saints, St. Faustina especially exemplifies the merciful. Jesus calls her the "secretary" of his mercy. Just as St. Thérèse of Lisieux encouraged the imperfect that it was possible to become saints, so Faustina encouraged the sinner to trust in God's mercy.

Faustina generously provided for the needs of the poor. She often forgave the sisters who calumniated her. And despite her intense sufferings, she would take on burdensome tasks for the community. Her prayer for mercy summarizes her interior dispositions toward those in need of mercy:

Help me, O Lord, that my eyes may be merciful, so that I may never suspect or judge from appearances, but look for what is beautiful in my neighbor's souls and come to their rescue. Help me, O Lord, that my ears may be merciful, so that I may give heed to my neighbor's needs and not be indifferent to their pains and moanings. Help me, O Lord, that my tongue may be merciful, so that I should never speak negatively of my neighbor, but have a word of comfort and forgiveness for all. Help me, O Lord, that my hands may be merciful and filled with good deeds, so that I may do only good to my neighbors and take upon myself the more difficult and toilsome tasks. Help me, O Lord, that my feet may be merciful, so that I may hurry to assist my neighbor, overcoming my own fatigue and weariness. My true rest is in the service of my neighbor. Help me, O Lord, that my heart may be merciful so that I myself may feel all the sufferings of my neighbor. I will refuse my heart to no one . . . O my Jesus, transform me into yourself, for you can do all things! Amen.[47]

To which gift and petition of the Our Father does this Beatitude correspond?

This Beatitude corresponds to the gift of *counsel*. St. Thomas points out, "It is a very good counsel against sin that a man gives alms and shows mercy."[48] For when a sinner seeks the most effective way to be freed from his sins and reunited to God, he finds that this most effective means is found in forgiving others and being merciful to others. Thus, Jesus says, "If you forgive men their trespasses, your heavenly Father also will forgive you" (Matt. 6:14). And again, "Give for alms those things which are within; and behold, everything is clean for you" (Luke 11:41). But the most complete teaching of Jesus on this point is found in a series of parables about mercy that Jesus tells in the Gospel according to Luke. In one of these parables, Jesus speaks about the usefulness of mercy:

There was a rich man who had a steward, and charges were brought to him that this man was wasting his goods. And he called him and said to him: "What is this that I hear about you? Turn in the account of your stewardship, for you can no longer be steward." And the steward said to himself: "What shall I do, since my master is taking the stewardship away from me? I am not strong enough to dig, and I am ashamed to beg. I have decided what to do, so that people may receive me into their houses when I am put out of the stewardship." So, summoning his master's debtors one by one, he said to the first: "How much do you owe my master?" He said: "A hundred measures of oil." And he said to him: "Take your bill, and sit down quickly and write fifty." Then he said to another: "And how much do you owe?" He said: "A hundred measures of wheat." He said to him: "Take your bill, and write eighty." The master commended the dishonest steward for his shrewdness; for the sons of this world are more shrewd in dealing with their own generation than the sons of light. And I tell you, make friends for yourselves by means of unrighteous mammon, so that when it fails they may receive you into the eternal habitations (Luke 16:1–9).

This parable teaches us how useful mercy is for our salvation. The rich master is God, who owns the world and all it holds. And since all the things we seem to have in this world are given to us by God, every man is a *steward* rather than the owner of his gifts. This is true even of the things that seem most of all to belong to a man: his own body and soul. In fact, God has a claim to ownership even of our bodies and souls on two counts: because he created us, and because he redeemed us. This is why St. Paul says, "For you have been purchased at a price. Therefore, glorify God in your body" (1 Cor. 6:12, NAB).

The steward in this parable signifies a man who has misused the gifts of God by his sins, and therefore deserves to be dismissed from God's service forever and cast into hell. But before this happens, the master calls him and says to him, "What is this that I hear about you? Turn in the account of your stewardship, for you can no longer be steward." Before the final judgment of each man, God calls out to him and warns him of his punishment. This call of God is the grace by which he makes us aware of our mortality and our sinfulness. And although it seems that his sentence has already been passed, each man is given the opportunity of accounting for his stewardship.

The truth is that none of us can change the past record of our stewardship: we can't make our past sins not be sins. But each of us can make amends for our past sins with the time we have left. And this is what the steward in the parable begins to deliberate about: how to make up for past sins. And the steward said within himself, "What shall I do, since my master is taking the stewardship away from me?" Here we see the gift of counsel at work. When a man sees the folly of seeking happiness in external goods, he withdraws from these external goods and begins to contemplate within his soul about what he must do. So just as the prodigal son returns to himself, so also the steward in this parable "says within himself" (Luke 16:3, DRA).

This *entering into ourselves* is a key moment in our conversion and return to God. St. Augustine speaks in the same way when he says, "You were within me, but I was outside, and it was there that I searched for you."[49] Our conversion begins by turning away from creatures and it ends by turning toward God, but between these two we must turn inward as an intermediate step. The Lord teaches this when he admonishes us, "What profit is there for one to gain the whole world yet lose or forfeit himself?" (Luke 9:25, NAB).

Since anyone who seeks happiness as an end must deliberate concerning the means to this end, so also a man who has lost the use of the goods in which he thought happiness would be found begins to deliberate about how to obtain the happiness he desires. For if we have changed the destination of our journey, we must also change the routes we choose to arrive there. So once again, the steward must use the gift of counsel to determine the appropriate means for obtaining forgiveness for his transgressions.

And first, he excludes two possibilities, saying, "I am not strong enough to dig, and I am ashamed to beg." To *dig* signifies the works of penance that are arduous and painful. For sometimes sinners make amends for their sins through great penances. But the steward considering his weakness rules this out. St. John Chrysostom speaks to sinners in this vein when he offers five paths to repentance for those who are weak.[50] To *beg* signifies prayers of petition and supplication, for sometimes sinners hope to obtain pardon by their prayers. But often it happens that one who is in sin considers that his prayers are not worthy to be heard. So the priest Ezra says, "My God, I am confounded and ashamed to lift up my face to thee: for our iniquities are multiplied over our heads, and our sins are grown up even unto heaven" (Ezra 9:6, DRA). And for this reason the steward rules out prayers of petition and supplication: "I am ashamed to beg." Therefore, he settles on a third means of obtaining the good he desires: to show mercy to the debtors of his master. This is the most powerful way recommended by the Lord himself: "Forgive us our sins, for we also forgive everyone that is indebted to us" (Luke 11:4, DRA).

Once someone has determined the appropriate means to the end that he desires, he proceeds to execute his plan. This, too, is the work of the gift of counsel. For contrition that does not bear fruit in action is not true contrition. He calls together "his master's debtors one by one" (the Greek says "each one of his master's debtors"). From this we learn two things about showing mercy through forgiveness: the steward does not wait for them to come to him, but calls them. So also, we must take the initiative to forgive. We can't say, "I will forgive only if they come to me begging." Secondly, his mercy is not restricted to one or a few, but extends to every one of his master's debtors. We too must forgive everyone, not just some.

To the first debtor who owed a hundred barrels of oil he says, "Take your bill, sit down quickly and write fifty." And to the second debtor who owed a hundred quarters of wheat he says, "Take your bill and write eighty." Oil and wheat ground into flour are the two ingredients the priests would use to make the bread of sacrifice (Lev. 2:4). The oil signifies mercy; the wheat ground into flour signifies contrition.

But what does it mean for the steward to write off debts owed to the master? I think this can be understood in several ways. First, it can mean forgiving them for the wrong they have done to us. For every sin against us is also a sin against God. And so the sin done by our neighbor against us is more a debt owed to God than to us. When we forgive them, in some sense we forgive part of that debt owed to God.

A second way this can be understood is that we are able to pay the debt of sin owed by another to God through our own resources. For just as in financial matters sometimes it happens that one man pays the debt of another man through mercy, so also this can happen in spiritual matters. St. Paul teaches that each Christian is able to remit the debt of another when he says: "In my flesh I am filling up what is lacking in the afflictions of Christ on behalf of his body, which is the church" (Col. 1:24, NAB). Therefore, sometimes God accepts the love of one of his friends offered for the sake of some sinner as if it had been offered by that sinner.

But neither of these explanations seems to be best, since it is clear in the parable that the steward pays the debt from the master's wealth rather than from his own. So I think it is better to understand this parable as referring to *indulgences*. And indulgence is the remission before God of the temporal punishment due to sins whose guilt has already been forgiven. The debt for this temporal punishment is paid from the excess merits of another, principally Christ. Understood in this way, the steward writes off the debts of his master's debtors using his master's own resources (i.e., the excess merits of Christ). And this fits best with the words of the parable.

So, the Lord is teaching us here that in our acts of mercy we ought to make use of indulgenced prayers and deeds as a privileged path to forgiveness of our own sins. Those who are liberated from purgatory on account of the indulgences we obtain for them will in their turn intercede for us from their "everlasting dwellings," that is, their places in heaven. By their prayers, God will free us from the guilt of our sins and the temporal punishment due to them.

There is another interpretation of this parable that applies specifically to priests and perhaps fits best of all with the words of the parable. For to priests has been granted the power to forgive sins through the sacrament of penance, and to atone for sins through the sacrifice of the Mass. Priests are especially stewards of the Lord, bearing his authority and representing him. And we are able to call the debtors of the Lord and write off their debts in a way that others cannot. When a priest absolves sins in the confessional, not only does he forgive the guilt of their sins, but the absolution remits some of the temporal punishment due to their sins as well. And when a priest says Mass for the souls of the faithful departed, he applies the atoning power of Calvary to the souls in purgatory to free them from their debt of punishment. Therefore, priests ought to take this parable of our Lord to heart and generously use the power given to them as a work of mercy. A priest is a spiritually rich man: not because of his own holiness, but because of the power given to him by Christ.

Jesus concludes the parable with the observation: "The master commended the dishonest steward for his shrewdness; for the sons of this world are more shrewd in dealing with their own generation than the sons of light." The gift of counsel is the gift by which we rightly determine and choose the best means to our ultimate end. The children of this world place their ultimate end in this world, whether it be in riches or pleasure or some other created good. And, for the most part, they are much better at finding and choosing the best means to these ends than the children of light are at finding and choosing the means to union with the uncreated God. For there are many who discover ingenious means and make great sacrifices for the sake of the earthly treasures they seek. But few are they who apply themselves with the same ingenuity or make great sacrifices for the kingdom of God, even among those who go by the name "Christian." We sacrifice much less for a much greater good, and so the children of this world are called wiser in their generation than the children of light.

Meditation on dishonest wealth

Jesus then gives a final exhortation about the utility of mercy when he says, "Make friends for yourselves with dishonest wealth, so that when it fails, you will be welcomed into eternal dwellings" (Luke 16:9, NAB).

If someone you knew gave you advice about how to make friends, and it involved money laundering, you just might wonder if you were getting the best advice! But the one giving advice in this case is someone you ought to listen to—even if he tells you to eat his flesh and drink his blood. So just how should we understand our Lord's advice about making friends with dishonest wealth? What is "dishonest wealth"? Luke gives three different scenarios in which wealth can be dishonest.

First, there is wealth obtained through unjust means. The tax collector Zacchaeus admits that he may have acquired some of his wealth in this way when he promises to restore four-fold anything he may have acquired through fraud (Luke 19). Another way in which wealth can be dishonest is when it is not shared with those in need. This happens in the case of the rich man and Lazarus, where the rich man does not use his wealth to help the beggar Lazarus at his door though he is in obvious need. But the third way in which wealth can be dishonest is the most subtle: when it is used as a substitute for trust in God's providence. This happened in the parable about the man who tore down his barns to build bigger ones (Luke 12). So in any of these ways we can be said to possess "dishonest wealth." Yet the Lord still provides us with a remedy if we find ourselves in possession of this kind of wealth.

Because wealth is a material good, it cannot be shared without being diminished. This is why wealth and other material goods tend to divide persons. On more than one occasion we read in the Gospel of Luke how the desire for an inheritance divides brothers. But there is a way in which material goods can unite persons: when they are given away. The act of love shown by giving others of our material possessions brings us together. And what is said about money in particular might be said more universally for any created good that someone can be said to possess: even our bodies or abilities.

Jesus says that we can make friends through dishonest wealth, and among the friends we can make is Jesus himself, who counts what we have done for the least of our brethren as done to him. What is truly beautiful is that Jesus accepts even dishonest wealth, things we have abused and misused: our possessions, our bodies, the powers of our soul. If we were to give such misused gifts, our dishonest wealth, to any self-respecting human sovereign, our gifts would be despised: "Your majesty, here is a car I used in a bank robbery; a knife I used in a murder; a platter I used for shoveling manure."

Yet, Jesus accepts praise from the lips we have used to rob our neighbor of his good reputation. He receives love from our hearts in which we murder our brother through anger; and from our members that we had dedicated to unchastity, he fashions a temple for his Holy Spirit. Jesus does not disdain them as something filthy when we turn and offer them to him and his service. How very good Jesus is. He does not behave like a self-respecting king, but like a poor beggar who takes whatever cheap trinkets we will give him. And yet after all this, we don't even give him the best of our tainted goods, but something less; and even that we give half-heartedly as if we were doing Jesus a favor. It ought not to be this way! It ought not to be this way!

In Luke's Gospel, we find an example of how Mary Magdalene changed the instruments of her harlotry into expressions of love and worship!

And behold, a woman of the city, who was a sinner, when she learned that he was sitting at table in the Pharisee's house, brought an alabaster flask of ointment, and standing behind him at his feet, weeping, she began to wet his feet with her tears, and wiped them with the hair of her head, and kissed his feet, and anointed them with the ointment . . . Then turning toward the woman [Jesus] said to Simon, "Do you see this woman? I entered your house, you gave me no water for my feet, but she has wet my feet with her tears and wiped them with her hair. You gave me no kiss, but from the time I came in she has not ceased to kiss my feet. You did not anoint my head with oil, but she has anointed my feet with ointment. Therefore I tell you, her sins, which are many, are forgiven, for she loved much" (7:37–47).

Jesus does not spurn her dishonest wealth. The hair and perfume with which she used to seduce men, even the lips with which she gave them unchaste kisses, have all been turned to the worship of the Savior.

We too have burdened ourselves with so much dishonest wealth, abused everything the Lord has given us. Let us hasten to unburden ourselves of so great a weight upon our consciences. Let us make friends with him who promised to go and prepare an everlasting dwelling for those who love him. Let us have confidence in his mercy and in the intercession of her who alone gave honest wealth to her son.

Forgive us our trespasses

Blessed are the merciful corresponds to the petition, "Forgive us our trespasses, as we forgive those who trespass against us." Forgiving sins is the ultimate way to show mercy, for sin is the ultimate misery, and mercy dispels misery.

The forgiveness of sins is due to the mercy of God, yet in all of God's works there is a kind of harmony between mercy and justice. Therefore, God shows mercy to us on the condition that we show mercy to our fellow man, so that a kind of justice is made manifest in God's mercy. In the parable of the creditor and his debtor, God says in the person of the creditor, "I forgave you all that debt because you besought me and should not you have had mercy on your fellow servant?" (Matt. 18:32–33).

Forgiveness is an act of mercy that makes us like our heavenly Father. The mystery of forgiveness is God's answer to the mystery of sin. In the beginning of his *Summa Theologiae,* St. Thomas raises an objection to the existence of God.[51] If God exists, the objection goes, he is infinite goodness. But if one of two contraries is infinite, the other would be totally destroyed. Therefore, since evil is contrary to good, and it is manifest that evil does exist in the world, it follows that infinite goodness cannot exist. Therefore, God does not exist.

It is a powerful objection, and probably the objection that lies at the root of nearly every atheist's disbelief. How does St. Thomas respond? He says that it belongs to God's infinite goodness to bring good even from evil, for there are many goods that could not exist unless evil existed. In other words, not every good is contrary to every evil. Some evils are the occasion of other goods. For example, unless there were physical evils like physical suffering and poverty, there could not be spiritual goods like patience in suffering and mercy in almsgiving. And since God sees that these spiritual goods far exceed the physical goods of health and wealth, he is willing to permit the evils of suffering and poverty, at least for a time.

But what about spiritual evils? What about sin? This is the greatest evil of all, so why would God allow it? It must be because God wills to bring about some greater good even out of sin itself. And so far as I can see, there are only three goods that could not exist unless sin existed. First is contrition or repentance. Yet contrition seems to more or less be equal to sin, to cancel it out. The second good is reparation for the sins of another, which goes beyond mere contrition. And the third good that cannot exist unless sin exists is forgiveness, and this seems not only to cancel out sin, but to surpass it. It is this good of forgiveness that I want to focus on here.

How beautiful a thing forgiveness is in the soul. It will be the most precious jewel in our heavenly crown. For the sake of drawing forgiveness from human hearts, God was willing to permit all the horrible crimes to which this fallen world is subject. God could have prevented Satan from entering the garden and deceiving our first parents. But he did not. God saw the world of Adam and Eve, all perfect and without sin, and it is as if he said to himself, "There is no forgiveness in that world. That is not the world I want. Better a world with sin and forgiveness than a world without sin and so without forgiveness." For he foresaw the beauty of forgiveness, and its beauty shone forth through the squalor of sin and transformed it into something glorious.

The Father especially foresaw the beauty of the final act of his Son from the cross when he forgave those who killed him, saying, "Father, forgive them!" By this one prayer from the lips of the Son, the whole world of sin was transformed from darkness into light. So, too, forgiveness shines through the filth of our own sins and transforms them: so much so that if a soul does only this one thing at the moment of death, if he will only forgive all those who have sinned against him, he will be admitted to paradise. Of all the petitions of the Our Father in Matthew's Gospel, the Lord chose to comment upon only this one when he solemnly attested: "If you will forgive men their offenses your heavenly Father will forgive you also your offenses but if you will not forgive men, neither will your Father forgive you your offenses" (Matt. 6:14–15, DRA).

It is very difficult to forgive. The jewels of forgiveness strewn along the paths of our lives are always found among thorns, and we must pay a price to grasp them. Yet pay that price we must. The whole reason why God has placed you in this fallen world instead of a perfect world untainted by sin is to draw forgiveness from your heart. And if you fail to forgive, your whole purpose for living and suffering in this world is in vain. Better a fallen sinful world with forgiveness than Eden without it. So, when the opportunity to forgive comes before you, say to yourself, "This is the moment! This is the reason why God has placed me in this fallen world! By this act of forgiveness I can make right so many sins and so much wrong."

There is a beautiful account of forgiveness in a book by Immaculée Ilibagiza called *Left to Tell*. It is the account of her life during the Rwandan genocide. She was hidden in a tiny bathroom with seven other women for three months as murderous bands roamed the countryside. Once she could hear the voices of some of her neighbors outside the bathroom window boasting how they had butchered her family. These were people who had been treated with kindness by her family, who had shared meals at their home. And so her heart was filled with hatred and bitterness.

In those dark days hidden away in her bathroom, Immaculée found comfort only in prayer, and she would say the rosary over and over, sometimes more than a dozen times each day. But whenever she said the Our Father, she would skip this petition *"forgive us our trespasses as we forgive those who trespass against us."* She could not pray those words because she could not find in her heart the strength to forgive. Yet each time she left them out, it stung her conscience. And then one day God gave her the miraculous gift of forgiveness and she was freed from the prison of her hatred and anger. Peace flooded her heart as she felt the freedom to once again say the Our Father in its fullness.

After she was liberated, she was brought to a prison camp where they dragged a man before her and threw him to the ground at her feet. They told her that he was one of the men who had killed her mother and brother, and they encouraged her to humiliate him. But instead she knelt down and embraced him and told him she forgave him. And the man wept tears of contrition. How beautiful a thing is forgiveness, but how great a price must often be paid for so noble a good.

When I lived in Rome for a time, I went down to Nettuno to visit the site of the martyrdom of St. Maria Goretti. She was the virgin martyr who resisted the violent assaults of a young man named Alessandro who tried to rape her, and ended by stabbing her to death. As she lay dying, she forgave him with all her heart. Later on, she appeared to him in his prison cell and he was converted. After he was released from prison, he became a brother in a friary and passed his life in penance and prayer.

But the most remarkable thing I saw on that trip to Nettuno was a photograph on the wall with an inscription indicating that the persons depicted were Alessandro and the mother of St. Maria Goretti peacefully sitting next to one another at her canonization.[52] What a miracle of grace that God should have given to that tender mother's heart, so deeply wounded, the gift of forgiveness for the man who murdered her daughter! That act of forgiveness by itself is sufficient proof of the existence of God and the truth of the Catholic faith.

Once, after giving a conference on forgiveness at a retreat, one of the priests said to me, "Father, you spoke beautifully on forgiveness, but what does it mean in the concrete to forgive? By what signs can we know that we have truly forgiven?" I thought much about that question, and although

I cannot say that I have a completely satisfactory answer, I will say this: we know we have forgiven perfectly if we treat the person we have forgiven the way we would want to be treated if we were the ones asking for forgiveness. And would you feel forgiven by God if he treated you the same way you treat those you have supposedly forgiven?

To put it more bluntly: if God never took the initiative in forgiving, would you feel forgiven by him? If God kept you at a distance and never again had a real conversation with you after you sinned, would you feel forgiven by him? If every time you sinned again, God held you guilty for all your past sins besides, would you feel that he really forgave you? If God refused ever again to say to you, "I love you," would you feel forgiven by him?

It is true that there are some relationships that are abusive and those where the offender does not even think he needs forgiveness. In cases like that, no real relationship is possible in this life, so all one can do is pray for someone like that to be converted, and this is enough. But I am talking about the many cases where someone who has deeply hurt you is sincerely sorry and comes asking for forgiveness. In such cases it is not enough to simply say, "I'll pray for you" and never speak to him again or never have a relationship with him again.

We cannot claim the gift of never having sinned. Innocence shall not be our plea before the judgment seat of Christ. Yet the mercies of the Lord are not exhausted, so long as we forgive as we have been forgiven. God has not been stingy with his mercy. If we refuse mercy to others, we have no excuse and we cast away our last, best hope for salvation.

There is one final point I want to make about this petition of the Our Father that applies specifically to priests. As ministers of reconciliation, God has given priests the power to forgive sins in his name. For the priest, therefore, *forgive us our sins as we forgive others* has special meaning. Priests have the opportunity to fulfill this command of the Lord not only in forgiving those who have sinned against us, but in forgiving those who have sinned against God and others. Priests who have been generous in hearing confessions shall receive the blessing reserved for the merciful: they shall receive mercy.

THE PURE OF HEART

Truly God is good to the upright,

to those who are pure in heart (Ps. 73:1).

Up until now, we have considered the Beatitudes that pertain to our private goods and our relationships with our fellow man. Now we ascend to the most perfect Beatitudes: those that touch immediately upon our relationship with God. And the first of these is, "Blessed are the pure of heart."

Who are the pure of heart?

When something is *pure*, it is unmixed with alien substances. Pure water does not have dirt in it, pure gold has no alloys. Something that is pure has *unity* and *integrity*. So what is a pure heart? A heart that *loves one thing*, with its entirety. Put briefly, a pure heart is one that keeps the first commandment: you shall love the Lord with all your heart.

We can also understand a pure heart by trying to understand pure *love*. Love is pure when it is directed toward something noble and good in such a way that it is not 1) self-interested, 2) half-hearted, or 3) clouded by some ulterior motive. So the pure of heart, as described in this Beatitude, love God in just this way. They love him for his own sake, not for something they can get from him. They love him with all their heart, so that nothing else competes with God as their object of love. And they love all other things, including themselves, for God's sake. Jesus implies the necessity for such purity of heart when he warns, "You cannot serve both God and mammon" (Matt. 6:24, Luke 16:13). And he implies the same thing when he says, "He who loves father or mother more than me is not worthy of me; and he who loves son or daughter more than me is not worthy of me" (Matt. 10:37).

The expression *purity of heart* also has a specific meaning pertaining to sexual purity. In this sense, the pure of heart are those who are not lustful; those who exhibit unity and integrity in their sexual appetite. Surely this disposition is necessary to love God rightly, but it does not seem to be the primary meaning of this expression when used in this Beatitude: for much more is necessary to see God than just being free from lust (for example, to see God the heart must also be free from hatred or unforgiveness).

What is their reward and how is it appropriate?

The reward for the pure of heart is that "they shall see God." This could mean with the eyes of the body or with the eye of the soul. Even those who were impure in heart beheld Christ with their bodily eyes as he walked upon this earth, and the wicked at the end of the world at the final judgment will do the same (Rev. 1:7). But only the just shall see him reigning in glory forever. Nevertheless, the primary sense of this reward is that the pure of heart will see the essence of God with the eye of the soul in the beatific vision: "We know that when he appears we shall be like him, for we shall see him as he is. And everyone who thus hopes in him purifies himself as he is pure" (1 John 3:2–3).

Yet it might seem that this reward is not appropriate. For clear vision seems to be a fitting reward for having a clean *eye* or *mind*, not a clean heart. Vision is an act of a knowing power, not a loving power.

But notice that an unclean heart can cause distorted vision. For this reason, Jesus says,

> Why do you see the speck that is in your brother's eye, but do not notice the log that is in your own eye? Or how can you say to your brother: "Let me take the speck out of your eye," when there is the log in your own eye? You hypocrite, first take the log out of your own eye, and then you will see clearly to take the speck out of your brother's eye (Matt. 7:3–5).

The *speck* and *log* here refer to sinful inclinations and desires. When our hearts are not pure, we cannot see reality clearly, especially reality concerning what is good and evil, right and wrong. We tend to overestimate the goodness of some things and underestimate the goodness of other things. Therefore, a pure heart is a prerequisite for seeing the divine goodness clearly.

Pope St. Leo the Great explains the appropriateness of this reward in this way: "Rightly is this blessedness promised to purity of heart. For the brightness of the true light will not be able to be seen by the unclean sight: and that which will be happiness to minds that are bright and clean, will be a punishment to those that are stained."[53] Here Leo explains why pure desires are needed in addition to unclouded sight. For even if we saw something clearly but we did not love what we saw, it would be more a cause of suffering than of joy. For example, for a man whose deeds are blameless it is delightful to know that God sees all things, but that same truth is a torment for those who do evil deeds and want those deeds to be hidden.

So, it is appropriate that one who loves with a pure heart should receive the object of that pure love as his reward. And the desire of a pure heart is to see God. Therefore, it is appropriate that the pure of heart should see God.

The example of Christ and the saints

Jesus had the purest of hearts: "He committed no sin, and no deceit was found in his mouth" (1 Pet. 2:22, NAB). When tested by the devil in the wilderness, he did not succumb in the least degree to his temptations. Therefore, St. Paul testifies, "For we have not a high priest who is unable to sympathize with our weaknesses, but one who in every respect has been tempted as we are, yet without sinning" (Heb. 4:15). And again, he says, "For it was fitting that we should have such a high priest, holy, blameless, unstained, separated from sinners, exalted above the heavens. He has no need, like those high priests, to offer sacrifices daily, first for his own sins and then for those of the people" (Heb. 7:26–27).

In all his desires, Jesus willed only to do the will of his Father: "The Son can do nothing of his own accord, but only what he sees the Father doing; for whatever he does, that the Son does likewise" (John 5:19). And his love for us was also most pure. He remained a virgin throughout his life. His desire was only to unite us to God his Father, and he laid down his life for us: "Greater love has no man than this: that a man lay down his life for his friends" (John 15:13).

After Jesus, the purest of hearts belonged to Our Lady. Her heart remained immaculate, unstained by any sin or bitterness or disordered desires. She pondered and kept in her heart the words and mysteries of the life of her son (Luke 2:19, 2:51). The words of Jesus found their most perfect expression in her: "As for that in the good soil, they are those who, hearing the word, hold it fast in an honest and good heart, and bring forth fruit with patience" (Luke 8:15). And even when she beheld her son crucified for our sins, she accepted us in the person of the beloved disciple as her own child in his place.

St. Thomas, too, deserves special mention in this regard. It was said at the end of his life, when he made his general confession, that his sins were those of a six-year-old child. He dedicated everything in his life to the love of God, praying and studying and teaching (to such a degree that by the end of his life he slept only half an hour each night). And he was known for his angelic purity, given to him as a special gift after he chased away a prostitute who was sent to seduce him while he was imprisoned. His purity of heart was so great that, near the end of his life, he received such a penetrating vision of God that some believe it was a momentary glimpse of the beatific vision itself.

Difficulties in living out this Beatitude

Living out this Beatitude demands that we live first by faith, not by sight. Even the Blessed Virgin Mary had to live and walk through the dark valley of faith in order to come to the bright day of vision. There were things about God and his plan for salvation that she did not understand at first

(Luke 1:34, 2:50). Yet, she accepted this plan with complete trust and in total faith, even when she beheld the fruit of her womb hanging from a tree. So even a heart untainted by original sin faced difficulty in living out this Beatitude. Much more do *our* hearts, infected as they are by original sin, struggle to live it out.

The first difficulty we have with living out this Beatitude is that *our hearts are inclined to sin*. Due to original sin, we are inclined to love creatures more than God and, in general, to love lesser goods more than greater ones. Therefore, the process of purifying our hearts is the work of divine grace. Once we receive divine grace through baptism, our hearts are enabled to love God above all things, and to love all things for his sake. Yet, this ability must be strengthened through repeated choices and deeds.

The principal means of purifying our hearts are the sacraments, prayer, and penance. The sacraments purify our hearts because they demand faith, communicating an increase of divine grace just from the fact that they are done according to the divine command.[54] Two sacraments in particular are useful as frequent means to attain greater purity of heart: penance and the Eucharist. The sacrament of penance purifies our hearts by our faith that God forgives our sins through the instrumentality of a mere man, and also by humbling us when we outwardly confess our sins. The sacrament of the Eucharist purifies us by requiring such great faith that we deny even the evident testimony of our senses to believe that Jesus Christ is truly and substantially present under the appearance of bread and wine. In the Eucharist, we come into contact with the Source of purity itself.

Prayer is also an essential means for purifying our hearts and minds. Since the pure heart must have God as the first and even sole object of its love, and since it is impossible to love someone without communion and regular conversation, it is impossible to be pure of heart without prayer. Prayer is conversation with God, and it unites the soul to God in a sweet communion.

The two dispositions most necessary for prayer are *perseverance* and *confidence*. Jesus teaches about each of these in Luke's Gospel, immediately after teaching his disciples the Our Father:

> Which of you who has a friend will go to him at midnight and say to him: "Friend, lend me three loaves; for a friend of mine has arrived on a journey, and I have nothing to set before him," and he will answer from within, "Do not bother me; the door is now shut, and my children are with me in bed; I cannot get up and give you anything?" I tell you, though he will not get up and give him anything because he is his friend, yet because of his importunity he will rise and give him whatever he needs. And I tell you, ask, and it will be given you; seek, and you will find; knock, and it will be opened to you. For every one who asks receives, and he who seeks finds, and to him who knocks it will be opened. What father among you, if his son asks for a fish, will instead of a fish give him a serpent; or if he asks for an egg, will give him a scorpion? If you then, who are evil, know how to give good gifts to your children, how much more will the heavenly Father give the Holy Spirit to those who ask him! (Luke 11:5–13).

In the parable, it is midnight—that is, it is the darkest hour of our life, when we cannot perceive God's truth or love. And we go to God in prayer asking to borrow three loaves. These three loaves signify the vision of the blessed Trinity: for the vision of God is for the soul what food is for the body. And yet, we seem to hear God rejecting us in this darkest of times. The door is locked—that is, Christ the door to heaven no longer grants access to the Father—and the children are in bed, that is, the saints are enjoying the eternal rest of heaven and seem to have no care for us. He cannot get up and give us anything; God cannot arise in our hearts to fulfill our longing.

During such times, when we seem to hear God tell us not to pray, we must remember that Jesus commands us to pray always, even if we seem to hear God rejecting us: "Pray always without becoming weary" (Luke 18:1, NAB). And so the parable concludes: even if he does not get up and give the man anything because of their friendship—that is, because we are in a state of grace—nevertheless, because of his perseverance the man will receive as much as he needs. We do not rely upon our goodness when we hope for good things from God, but upon *his* goodness. And, therefore, we can hope for great things indeed!

This parable teaches us about the importance of perseverance in prayer: that all who persevere will receive from God everything they need to be saved. This perseverance, more than anything, purifies our hearts and makes them clean in God's eyes.

Finally, *penance* also purifies our hearts. St. John of the Cross, St. Anthony Mary Claret, St. Rose of Lima, and many others testify that it is impossible to become holy without voluntary, bodily mortification. As Paul testifies, the flesh wars against the spirit, and the spirit against the flesh (Gal. 5:17). If the spirit does not fight against the inclinations of the flesh, the flesh begins to conquer parts of our heart, leading us to love sensible pleasures more than spiritual goods. Therefore, we must do voluntary penance in order to keep our hearts pure from the dominion of the flesh.

Besides these active works of purification, the soul must also undergo *passive* purifications in order for us to have a truly pure heart. They are called passive because God is the sole agent of these purifications: we can only cooperate passively by undergoing these trials patiently. God cleans our hearts in ways that no effort on our part could accomplish, but these deep cleanings of our heart are very painful. An example of these passive purifications is explained by the saints as "dark nights," and their classic doctrine is given in the writings of St. John of the Cross.

The first of these dark nights is the dark night of the *senses*, where we lose every sensible consolation of God's presence. We feel rejected by God and the thought of spiritual works like prayer are loathsome to the soul. In such times, we are given the opportunity to do works of love and worship even though we feel no incentive or reward. On the contrary, we feel positively punished for doing them. Yet we are enabled to do these works in such a way that seems to bring no benefit to ourselves. This manifests that our love for God is pure and not tainted by self-love.

The second of these dark nights is called the dark night of the *spirit*, and it is characterized especially by temptations against faith. During such times, the teachings of Christ and his Church seem to be nonsense, and obviously false. Our whole reason for becoming Christian and remaining Christian seems to be taken away. God does this so that our faith will not stand upon any human rationale but solely upon his power and promise. For so long as our belief makes sense to us, we cannot be sure if we accept it based upon our own judgments or upon God's word. But a soul who has passed through this dark night of the spirit is purified to such a degree that he becomes certain that his faith rests upon God alone, not upon his own views of what seems reasonable to him.

Although both of these passive purifications are very painful and terrifying, God supports the generous soul through such trials. They are necessary to purify the heart beyond what is possible through human effort. And the soul who successfully passes through them is truly prepared to see God.

To which gift and petition of the Our Father does this Beatitude correspond?

This Beatitude corresponds to the gift of *understanding*, which is to the mind what sight is to the eye. Just as one who has a clean eye sees physical things clearly, so one who has his mind purified by the gift of understanding sees the truths about God. Thus, St. John asserts, "We know that when he appears we shall be like him, for we shall see him as he is. And everyone who thus hopes in him purifies himself as he is pure" (1 John 3:2–3).

The gift of understanding makes someone see clearly and without darkness those things that are of faith. In her diary, St. Faustina describes her own experience of this gift:

> The great light which illumines the mind gives me a knowledge of the greatness of God; but it is not as if I were getting to know the individual attributes, as before—no, it is different now: in one moment, I come to know the entire essence of God.
>
> In that same moment, the soul drowns entirely in him and experiences a happiness as great as that of the chosen ones in heaven. Although the chosen ones in heaven see God face to face and are completely and absolutely happy, still their knowledge of God is not the same. God has given me to understand this. This deeper knowledge

begins here on earth, depending on the grace [given], but to a great extent it also depends on our faithfulness to that grace. However, the soul receiving this unprecedented grace of union with God cannot say that it sees God face to face, because even here there is a very thin veil of faith, but so very thin that the soul can say that it sees God and talks with him. It is "divinized."[55]

This understanding of God and the truths about God are not the result of mere study as if a course in theology could produce this effect. Rather, this penetration of understanding is the result of a heart purified from earthly desires. In order to arrive at this clarity of vision, it is necessary first to pass through the darkness of faith.

This Beatitude also corresponds to the petition, "Lead us not into temptation." For those who are led into temptation have a divided heart. St. Thomas says succinctly, "If [the gift of] understanding is that by which the blessed are pure of heart, then we pray that we might not have a double heart, by pursuing temporal goods, about which temptations arise within us."[56]

It can be difficult to understand the precise sense of this petition. For what exactly are we praying? St. James says, "[God] himself tempts no one" (James 1:13). So why should we pray for something that will happen whether or not we pray for it? It is true that God does not incline our hearts to sin, yet he does sometimes withdraw his grace when a man, through his ingratitude or abuse of God's gifts, merits to have them removed. It is in this sense that we ask God not to lead us into temptation.

But there is another difficulty. It seems that temptation is sometimes good. For example, James writes, "Count it all joy, when you shall fall into diverse temptations" (James 1:2,

DRA). So it seems that we should ask God *to* lead us into temptation. St. Thomas and St. Augustine teach that when we pray this petition we do not ask to be freed from testing and trials (for these are the necessary occasions of perfection in virtue) but rather from being tested *beyond our strength* and being *overcome* by these trials.

In fact, it must be said that the entire reason God permits evil in the world is so that the saints might manifest a virtue and perfection greater than that which would have existed were there no evil in the world. For the love of the saints was never so great as when they forgave their murderers in the very act of murder. And such a love would hardly have been possible had God not permitted evil men to persecute his holy ones. This is why Jesus says, "If you love those who love you, what reward have you?" (Matt. 5:46). And in the Psalms we read, "The anger of men shall serve to praise you; its survivors surround you with joy" (76:10, ICEL). And so when we pray this petition, we do not ask that God take away all trials (since these are for our good); nor do we ask God not to incline our hearts to sin (for this he would never do); but we ask that God not withdraw his grace that preserves us from sin, and that he give us strength to overcome the trials he permits to befall us.

In this way, our hearts become pure. For we neither desire comfort nor trials in themselves but rather we desire them to the degree that they are beneficial for our salvation and the common good. Thus, our hearts are fixed upon one desire: that God's will be done so that his grace may triumph in us according to his plan for our salvation.

9

THE PEACEMAKERS

The fear of the Lord is the crown of wisdom,

making peace and perfect health to flourish (Sir. 1:18).

St. Thomas connects this seventh Beatitude with the sixth by pointing out that both are effects of the active life disposing for the contemplative life. But the sixth Beatitude pertains to a man's perfection in himself, whereas the seventh Beatitude pertains to a man's perfection in relation to his *neighbors*:

> Now the effect of the active life, as regards those virtues and gifts whereby man is perfected in himself [so as to be disposed for the contemplative life], is the cleansing of man's heart, so that it is not defiled by the passions: hence the sixth Beatitude is: "Blessed are the clean of heart." But as regards the virtues and gifts whereby man is perfected in relation to his neighbor, the effect of the active life is peace, according to Isaiah 32:17: "The work of justice shall be peace." Hence the seventh Beatitude is "Blessed are the peacemakers."[57]

In other words, virtues such as temperance and fortitude and meekness, as well as the corresponding gifts of the Holy Spirit, purify a man's heart in such a way that he is able to live a life of quiet union with God in knowledge, love, and prayer, without the disturbance of unruly passions. On the other hand, those virtues and their corresponding gifts dispose the soul in such a way that a man is enabled to live in peace with his neighbors, and even is enabled to make peace within his community so that others might also live lives of contemplation and union with God. This common life of contemplation of divine things is the highest peace. Therefore, we can more easily see how the sixth Beatitude, "Blessed are the pure of heart," is presupposed to this seventh Beatitude.

Who are the peacemakers?

The first attribute of peace that is well known to everyone is that it involves the absence of conflict and strife. It is easy to know when there is not peace. Because of this, many people simply identify peace with an absence of fighting and conflict. Often we are told that we should just get along, and not rock the boat. This is a false peace. As Bl. Pier Giorgio Frassati once wrote in a letter to a friend, "To live without faith, without a heritage to defend, without battling constantly for truth, is not to live, but to 'get along.' We must never just 'get along.'"

Just because there is no outward fighting does not mean there is no internal tension and division. The years under Pope St. John Paul II and Pope Benedict XVI had very little outward fighting among bishops, but now we see that there was much internal division and tension present. Many bishops had been hiding their true ideas and agendas, and that hidden disorder is now manifesting itself in the modern Church with fighting and dissension.

So peace requires an interior ordering. Once this right order is established, tranquility results and there is a lasting and stable resting in the good. This peace, in turn, disposes men for living the contemplative life, and ultimately disposes us for the contemplative life of heaven. So the peacemaker is one who addresses the root of the problem: he moves hearts and minds to be rightly ordered in themselves, in relation to others, and in relation to God. This obviously presupposes both wisdom and charity.

Every virtuous person can see this need for right order and peace; and every virtuous person can work for it. But when inspired by the gifts of the Holy Spirit, someone is so ardently inflamed by a desire to make peace and so enlightened by the Holy Spirit, he produces effects beyond the power of nature. In his own person, he absorbs the effects of sin and disorder; he makes reparation and offers forgiveness. He does not return insult for insult, but a blessing instead.

This is why Scripture says of the peacemaker: "When a man's ways please the Lord, he makes even his enemies to be at peace with him" (Prov. 16:7). Not only this, but due to the supernatural light of divine wisdom he can see a way to restore and preserve order that is not apparent to others. It belongs to the wise man to preserve order precisely because he sees the right order better than others. He sees solutions to conflict that others overlook. He penetrates into the deeper motives of human hearts, and can therefore move those hearts more effectively toward the good.

What is their reward and why is it appropriate?

The reward for those who make peace is that "they will be called sons of God." Who will call them sons of God? God himself will call them his children.[58] And since God makes all things to be by his word, by calling them his children, they shall be his children: "He spoke and it came to be" (Ps. 33:9). They shall also be called sons of God by the angels, who are also called sons of God in Scripture (for example: Job 1:5, 2:1; and Luke 20:36). For the angels were also peacemakers, since at the birth of Christ they proclaimed peace on earth. Finally, other men shall call the peacemakers sons of God. For establishing peace is more a divine than a human work.

It is appropriate that God call the peacemakers his sons, for a number of reasons. First, because they bear a likeness to his natural Son, Jesus Christ, who established peace between God and man (Col. 1:20), between Jew and Gentile (Eph. 2:12–22), and among all men (John 14:27). They are also called children of God because they imitate God's own work. For just as God established peace by setting the world in order, so too do peacemakers reestablish the original order and peace instituted by God. Again, it is appropriate that the peacemakers be called sons of God because they establish peace by forgiving the sins of others and by making reparation for those sins. In this they are like God who also forgives our sins, and who became a man to make reparation for our sins.

Finally, it is appropriate that the peacemakers are called sons of God because they help to bring about union between God and their fellow man. Therefore, the peacemakers should be rewarded with the greatest possible union with God—being united to God as his own children. St. Thomas gives this reason: "To make peace either in oneself or among others, shows a man to be an imitator of God, Who is the God of unity and peace. Hence, as a reward, he is promised the glory of the divine sonship, consisting in perfect union with God through consummate wisdom."[59]

It is also appropriate that the holy angels call the peacemakers sons of God. For in making peace between God and men, they are like the angels: "Suddenly there was with the angel a multitude of the heavenly host praising God and saying: 'Glory to God in the highest, and on earth peace among men with whom he is pleased!'" (Luke 2:13–14). Moreover, the angels assist God in the divine governance of the world, and so they are instrumental in bringing about order, harmony, and peace.

Finally, it is appropriate that the peacemakers are called sons of God by other men. For a son proceeds from his father and bears a specific likeness to his father. But those who make peace proceed from God. This is why Jesus says after his resurrection, "Peace be with you. As the Father has sent me, even so I send you" (John 20:21). That is, men are able to make peace because they are sent by the natural Son of God and proceed from him. And they have a specific likeness to God, insofar as it is proper to God to forgive sins, yet he has shared this power with men: "If you forgive the sins of any, they are forgiven; if you retain the sins of any, they are retained" (John 20:23; cf. Matt. 9:8). This is why priests are called sons of God in a special way: they establish peace through the offering of the sacrifice of the Mass and the forgiveness of sins in the sacrament of confession.

There is still another reason why the peacemakers should be called sons of God. As we shall see below, the gift corresponding to this Beatitude is the gift of wisdom. And the natural Son of God proceeds as wisdom from the Father. So also, those who have the gift of wisdom are like the natural Son in a special manner. For all of these reasons, and many more besides, it is appropriate that the peacemakers be called sons of God.

How can we become peacemakers?

Becoming and being a peacemaker is toward the end of our spiritual journey. Therefore, we should not be anxious if we are not able to be peacemakers right from the beginning of our own conversion. Weightlifters do not expect to lift the heaviest weights at the beginning of their training, but at the end. So too, we must recognize that being able to establish peace among others requires great maturity in the spiritual life.

That being said, there are four major steps in order to become a peacemaker.

The first step is that we must establish *peace within ourselves*. If we are not at peace with ourselves, we will not be at peace with others. To be at peace within ourselves, we must establish right order in our souls, and this begins with truth. We must rightly understand the truths of the faith and grow in wisdom. If our souls are filled with error and ignorance, we will not be able to tell what is right or wrong, or what is good or bad. Therefore, we must learn to love the scriptures, and to be docile to the teaching of Christ and his apostles as transmitted through the Church. After this, we must put ourselves in a right relationship with God by confessing our sins and worshiping him as he has commanded. Finally, we must train our passions by keeping the commandments, mortification, and selfless choices. If our passions are not at peace and subject to our reason, we will not have peace within ourselves.

The second major step in becoming a peacemaker is to patiently *bear the burdens of others*. This step is recommended by St. Paul:

> But the fruit of the Spirit is love, joy, peace, patience, kindness, goodness, faithfulness, gentleness, self-control; against such there is no law. And those who belong to Christ Jesus have crucified the flesh with its passions and desires. If we live by the Spirit, let us also walk by the Spirit. Let us have no self-conceit, no provoking of one

another, no envy of one another. Brethren, if a man is overtaken in any trespass, you who are spiritual should restore him in a spirit of gentleness. Look to yourself, lest you too be tempted. Bear one another's burdens, and so fulfill the law of Christ (Gal. 5:22–6:2).

Bearing one another's burdens is indispensable for establishing peace. For if we are constantly agitated at the weaknesses of others and refuse to put up with them, we will begin to provoke fights by demanding of our brothers things that they are not always strong enough to accomplish. And although Jesus was always very harsh with those who committed sins from malice (such as the Pharisees), he was always very gentle with those who sinned from weakness or ignorance. St. Paul recommends this method with those whose faith is weak:

I know and am persuaded in the Lord Jesus that nothing is unclean in itself; but it is unclean for anyone who thinks it unclean. If your brother is being injured by what you eat, you are no longer walking in love. Do not let what you eat cause the ruin of one for whom Christ died. So do not let your good be spoken of as evil. For the kingdom of God is not food and drink but righteousness and peace and joy in the Holy Spirit. He who thus serves Christ is acceptable to God and approved by men. Let us then pursue what makes for peace and for mutual upbuilding. Do not, for the sake of food, destroy the work of God. Everything is indeed clean, but it is wrong for anyone to make others fall by what he eats (Rom. 14:14–20).

The question is not who is right or wrong. It's true that those whose faith was weak were wrong about the uncleanness of certain kinds of food. Yet Paul does not instruct the Romans to simply tell them that they are wrong and to get over it. Rather, he recommends that those whose faith is strong bear with the inconvenience of not eating certain foods so as not to scandalize the others. This is striking advice, since it manifests that in moral matters it is not merely a question of what is the objective truth—but also whether or not we *care* about those who may be in error and whose error cannot be remedied immediately.

The third major step in becoming a peacemaker is *fraternal correction*. The book of Proverbs teaches: "He who winks the eye causes trouble, but he who boldly reproves makes peace" (Prov. 10:10). Our Lord gives very concrete steps for offering fraternal correction, and St. Augustine, in his rule of life, amplifies and explains these steps.

> If your brother sins against you, go and tell him his fault, between you and him alone. If he listens to you, you have gained your brother. But if he does not listen, take one or two others along with you, that every word may be confirmed by the evidence of two or three witnesses. If he refuses to listen to them, tell it to the church; and if he refuses to listen even to the church, let him be to you as a Gentile and a tax collector (Matt. 18:15–17).

The first step in fraternal correction is that you should be a witness to or somehow certain of the sin. If you are not certain, it belongs to someone else to make the correction. The next step is to go to the person alone. For we should be very sensitive to preserving the good name of others. A good name is more valuable than gold or precious perfume (Prov. 22:1 and Eccl. 7:1), so taking it away is worse than stealing. Indeed, even bad people deserve a good name among those whom they have not harmed or are not likely to harm. Notice that in this step the purpose is not to defend yourself but rather to "gain your brother." We correct the sins of others not because we are hurt, but because it is not good for them to sin. Therefore, fraternal correction is an act of love, and it should be done in such a way that the one being corrected can feel loved by the one correcting.

If he does not listen, the next step is to bring along two or three others. Sometimes a person will not admit that he has sinned because he simply disagrees with you about whether there was a sin in the first place. Or perhaps he cannot take a correction well because he has been hurt by you in the past and does not believe you are objective. By bringing witnesses, you introduce a measure of objectivity into the process.

Last of all, if the person will not accept the correction from two or three brethren, he should be brought before the authority of the whole Church, so that he might know for certain that his action was sinful and cannot be tolerated within the communion of the Church. Obviously, such cases should be serious: things like heresy or schism, or sins that make peace impossible within the Church such as public impurity, murder, theft, and so on. (Less serious matters— irascibility, talkativeness, laziness, etc.—often must be borne with.) If he will not repent even after this, he must be excluded from the communion of the Church. And this, too, is done from love, lest his contagious corruption ruin others.[60]

Clearly, such fraternal correction presupposes that you are not guilty of the same or worse sins! Jesus himself warned,

> Why do you see the speck that is in your brother's eye, but do not notice the log that is in your own eye? Or how can you say to your brother: "Let me take the speck out of your eye," when there is the log in your own eye? You

hypocrite, first take the log out of your own eye, and then you will see clearly to take the speck out of your brother's eye (Matt. 7:3–5).

So, in summary, fraternal correction should be done 1) by one whose place it is to make the correction, 2) with love, and 3) without hypocrisy.

The last step in becoming a peacemaker is *forgiveness and reparation*. When someone sins against us or the common good, harm is done to us. The natural tendency is to harm him back so he knows firsthand what he has done to us and to others. But this is not how Jesus treated us. When Jesus saw humanity's sins, he did not think first, "How can I hurt or punish them?" Rather, he thought, "How can I take their punishment upon myself to save and help them?" As St. Faustina observed, we should be more willing to do penance for the sins of others than to punish them.

There is an old saying: "Forgiveness means somebody takes the loss." By forgiving and making reparation for the sins of others, we absorb in our own persons the evil others have done. Yet by this very act we are made holy and beautiful in God's eyes. So we suffer no real loss and achieve great gains. Yet it requires great courage to endure so much pain without building a wall around our hearts to protect them. The hearts of Jesus and Mary are always depicted as wounded for precisely this reason.

The example of Christ and the saints

Jesus came to give us peace as he testified, "Peace I leave with you; my peace I give to you; not as the world gives do I give to you" (John 14:27). He came to share the unity and peace shared among the three Persons of the Most Holy

Trinity: "That they may all be one; even as thou, Father, art in me, and I in thee, that they also may be in us" (John 17:21). And when he became man, he reestablished right order and peace. He did this first through his wise teaching, which set all truth in order and removed all error. Then, through his cross, he suffered the effects of all the disorder of all the sins committed in the history of the world and made atonement for those sins:

> In him all the fullness of God was pleased to dwell, and through him to reconcile to himself all things, whether on earth or in heaven, making peace by the blood of his cross. And you, who once were estranged and hostile in mind, doing evil deeds, he has now reconciled in his body of flesh by his death, in order to present you holy and blameless and irreproachable before him (Col. 1:19–22).

He also brought about peace between Gentiles and Jews, by inviting the pagan nations to be grafted upon the true tree of life:

> For he is our peace, who has made us both one, and has broken down the dividing wall of hostility, by abolishing in his flesh the law of commandments and ordinances, that he might create in himself one new man in place of the two, so making peace, and might reconcile us both to God in one body through the cross, thereby bringing the hostility to an end. And he came and preached peace to you who were far off and peace to those who were near; for through him we both have access in one Spirit to the Father. So then you are no longer strangers and sojourners, but you are fellow citizens with the saints and members of the household of God (Eph. 2:14–19).

Finally, at the end of time, Jesus will come in glory to establish a final and definitive justice and peace: "Now the salvation and the power and the kingdom of our God and the authority of his Christ have come" (Rev. 12:10). So Jesus Christ is the supreme peacemaker.

What, then, are we to make of Jesus' own words when he said, "Do you think that I have come to establish peace on the earth? No, I tell you, but rather division" (Luke 12:51)?

The word *peace*, like *love* and *good*, has many meanings. Sometimes it refers to a merely apparent peace, as when thieves are at peace with one another because they are working together to commit a crime. At other times it refers to a limited peace, such as that enjoyed between two people who are friends because they enjoy the same amusements. Such peace is transient and quickly disappears in the face of more important matters. For such a friendship would easily dissolve if one of them insulted or harmed the family of the other. But Jesus came to establish a true and eternal peace, founded upon an immovable rock. Pope St. Leo the Great explains this distinction between false or earthly peace and the peace our Lord came to bring:

> This blessedness, beloved, belongs not to any and every kind of agreement and harmony, but to that of which the apostle speaks: have peace toward God, and of which the prophet David speaks: much peace have they that love your law, and they have no cause of offenses. This peace even the closest ties of friendship and the most exact likeness of mind do not really gain, if they do not agree with God's will. Similarity of bad desires, leagues in crimes, associations of vice, cannot merit this peace.[61]

Every peace is the result of order, and some kinds of order are more profound and lasting than others.[62] Jesus came to reestablish the right order between God and creation, which is the most fundamental order that exists. And any order that is not in harmony with that order must be supplanted. Even the family order based upon human generation must be subordinated to the order established by God in the act of creation. So, the true peace established by Christ requires *division and separation*: of light from darkness, of truth from error, of good men from evil men. Only then can true and lasting peace be established. This is why Jesus says he came to bring division: so that through this division a true and lasting unity and peace might be established.

Among the saints, the Blessed Virgin Mary is the greatest peacemaker. She is the new Eve who untied the knot and reversed the disorder caused by the first Eve. Whereas the first Eve plucked the fruit from the tree of the knowledge of good and evil, Mary consented to leave the fruit of her womb upon the cross, the tree of the knowledge of God's goodness and man's evil. In this way she absorbed into herself the evil caused by original sin and caused peace to reign once again.

Another saint notable for being a peacemaker is St. Thomas Aquinas. In his time, there was great disagreement among theologians and between theologians and philosophers. Even basic questions like how many sacraments are there were still being debated. And the teaching of Aristotle was considered by many to be fundamentally in conflict with divine revelation. St. Thomas, through his great wisdom, was able to convincingly demonstrate the right order of causes in both philosophy and theology and, by so doing, established peace between these most noble sciences.

Finally, St. Norbert deserves mention among the great peacemakers in the history of the Church. His vocation to make peace was evident at his conversion. As he was on a journey, lightning struck the earth right in front of the horse he was riding, knocking him senseless to the ground: "Coming to himself he was touched with grief of heart and began to say to himself: 'Lord what do you want me to do?' Immediately, as if God were responding [he heard]: 'Turn from evil and do good; seek peace and pursue it.'"[63]

At a time when factions among Christian princes were warring ceaselessly, Norbert would travel from town to town bringing about reconciliation between rival princes and families. He did this especially through his preaching of forgiveness and the offering of the Holy Mass. He was so successful that he was called the apostle and angel of peace.

To which gift and petition of the Our Father does this Beatitude correspond?

As we have already seen above, this Beatitude corresponds to the gift of *wisdom*. The reason for this is clear once we see the relationship between order, wisdom, and peace. Wisdom establishes right order, whereas peace is an *effect* of right order. The wise man is able to understand and judge the right order among causes. He is, therefore, in a position to make peace. From the order within his own soul, he is able to introduce right order in the things around him. This order is not merely an order among truths, but also an order of love and of relationships. The apostle James teaches, "The wisdom from above is first pure, then peaceable, gentle, open to reason, full of mercy and good fruits, without uncertainty or insincerity. And the harvest of righteousness is sown in peace by those who make peace" (James 3:17–18).

It is by wisdom, too, that we are made children of God: "Give me wisdom, the attendant at your throne, and reject me not from among your children" (Wis. 9:4, NAB). For wisdom conforms us to that Wisdom who is the very Son of God. And those who are children of the Blessed Virgin Mary, whom the Church calls "wisdom" in her liturgy, are also made children of God.

The petition of the Our Father, "Deliver us from evil" corresponds to the Beatitude "blessed are the peacemakers." St. Thomas explains it this way:

> God frees man from evil and temptations by converting them into something good, which is a sign of the greatest wisdom. For someone wise is able to ordain even evil to some good purpose. And this is accomplished through patience, which is possessed during tribulations. For the other virtues make use of goods, but patience makes use of evils . . . And, therefore, through the gift of wisdom, the Holy Spirit causes us to ask [that we be delivered from evil]. And through this we arrive at beatitude: that beatitude which is an effect of the order established in peace. For through patience we have peace in times of prosperity and adversity. And so the peacemakers are called "sons of God" because they are like God, since just as nothing is able to harm God, so neither is anything able to harm them, either in prosperity or adversity.[64]

Those who are wise are so established in peace, so firmly founded upon right order, that, like an immovable rock, they are unable to be moved or harmed in any way. And so they are delivered from every evil. Such a peace was found in the soul of Christ, even as he hung upon the cross. This consideration leads us to the final Beatitude.

10

THOSE WHO ARE PERSECUTED FOR THE SAKE OF RIGHTEOUSNESS

Why is there an eighth Beatitude?

Based upon what we have seen so far, the previous seven Beatitudes seem to be complete. The rewards promised seem to
have their culmination in universal peace and membership in
the family of God. The correspondence of each Beatitude to
the seven gifts of the Holy Spirit and seven petitions of the Our
Father also seem to indicate that seven Beatitudes are enough.
Yet our Lord adds this eighth Beatitude. Why does he do this?

In response to this objection, St. Thomas explains:

The eighth Beatitude is a certain confirmation aed mani-
festation of all the preceding Beatitudes. For from the fact

that someone is confirmed in poverty of spirit, and meekness, and all the others, the result is that he will not depart from any of these goods on account of any persecution. Hence, in a certain way, the eighth Beatitude pertains to the preceding seven.[65]

St. Thomas points out that being made firm in the Beatitudes is itself an additional reason for joy. If someone gave you a beautiful new mansion you would probably be glad. But if there were some fear that you could lose it, that would certainly temper your joy. It would be a much greater cause for joy if you got the mansion together with an assurance that it could not be taken away and you could always live there. Similarly, if the woman or man of your dreams were in love with you, you would certainly be happy about that. But if you married this person, the stability of the relationship would be an even greater cause for joy.

So too, with this eighth Beatitude, the very fact that it indicates a stability and permanence in the other seven is an even greater cause for joy, which is why the Lord Jesus pronounces *twice* blessed those who suffer persecution for the sake of righteousness.

St. Paul speaks about this state of permanent union with God, and the blessings it affords:

Who shall separate us from the love of Christ? Shall tribulation, or distress, or persecution, or famine, or nakedness, or peril, or sword? As it is written: "For thy sake we are being killed all the day long; we are regarded as sheep to be slaughtered." No, in all these things we are more than conquerors through him who loved us. For I am sure that neither death, nor life, nor angels, nor principalities, nor things present, nor things to come, nor powers, nor height, nor depth, nor anything else in all creation, will be able to separate us from the love of God in Christ Jesus our Lord (Rom. 8:35–39).

To be confirmed in God's love is already to begin to live the life of heaven while on earth.

There is another reason why this eighth Beatitude should be a cause of the greatest joy. Jesus implies this reason when he explains this Beatitude in greater detail. He says, "In the same way they persecuted the prophets who were before you." By enduring persecution for the sake of righteousness, we are *made like the prophets*. Thus, it is a certification that we have been sent by God and that we are divinely chosen instruments for the dissemination of the Gospel.

So, our happiness goes beyond the happiness of one who possesses Christ. It is also the happiness of one who brings Christ to the whole of God's people. The one who suffers persecution for the sake of righteousness becomes an effectual bearer of Christ to the souls of others, even to the hard of heart. For just as St. Stephen's martyrdom was intimately linked to the conversion of Saul, so too will our fidelity in persecution be the means by which grace is communicated to the hearts of the unrepentant.

Finally, there is one more reason why the Lord Jesus should have added this eighth Beatitude. There were seven days of creation that at first seemed complete. Yet, after man sinned, it was necessary for there to be an eighth day, the day of the resurrection, in order to recreate the whole cosmos. So too, the Lord adds an eighth Beatitude that reflects the Pascal mystery: the death and resurrection of the Lord. The day of the Sabbath, the day on which peace is made, corresponds to the seventh Beatitude. Yet this day is superseded by the true Sabbath, the day in which man is recreated and set firmly at rest in God.

So we can see why the Lord Jesus includes this last Beatitude above and beyond the seven he has already given. Eight is enough.

Who are those who are persecuted?

This eighth Beatitude is, "Blessed are those who are persecuted for the sake of righteousness, for theirs is the kingdom of heaven." What does it mean to be persecuted for the sake of righteousness?

First of all, it does not mean anyone who suffers persecution for any reason, but only those who suffer persecution for a good cause, such as truth or virtue, and especially justice. And persecution means not just any evil or punishment, but an evil brought about by men who intend to prevent you from saying or doing the right thing. Furthermore, persecution implies a certain kind of persistence in their attempts to harm you. For it implies that you are being pursued or followed by your persecutors. They are not content to let you continue to live a good life elsewhere.

What are the stages of persecution? Jesus himself answers this question when he adds in the following verse, "Happy are you when men reproach you, and persecute you, and, lying, say every wicked thing about you." Here Jesus identifies three elements to being persecuted for the sake of righteousness.

First, you are *reproached*. The Greek word here has the sense of "giving someone a bad name." That is, you are publicly accused of moral fault. Second, you are *persecuted*. The Greek word here has the sense of "being driven away" or "pursued with punishment." Third, men *lie and say every wicked thing about you*. That is, once they have defamed you, and pursued you, they falsely accuse you of every wicked deed in order to bring about your final demise. This was the method used by the Sadducees, Pharisees, and scribes against Jesus. First they defamed him to the crowds. Then they pursued and harassed him. And finally, they lied in court about him and accused him of every wicked deed to bring about his crucifixion and death.

What is their reward and why is it appropriate?

The reward for those who are persecuted is "the kingdom of heaven." This is the exact same description of the reward offered to those who are poor in spirit. Above we have considered the reasons for this, but this is a good place to revisit those considerations.

The first point to acknowledge is that by describing the reward in identical terms, Jesus is showing a kind of unity among all the rewards of the Beatitudes. For all of them in some way refer to the possession of God as a final reward. If the first and last Beatitudes have the same reward, this implies that all the ones in between also have the same reward. It also calls to mind the teaching of Jesus that the first shall be last and the last shall be first. For example, all those who worked, whether for the whole day or even for the last hour, were given the same wage (Matt. 20:1–13).

But that same reward is described in different terms throughout the other Beatitudes, which implies that here is something new; some new aspect under which this last reward implies some perfection beyond that described in the first Beatitude. And if we recall that the sixth and seventh Beatitudes describe our eternal reward as a kind of contemplative possession of God, it makes sense that this eighth Beatitude should also be understood in this way.

The sixth Beatitude describes the reward as seeing God. This is an act of contemplative possession, an act by which an individual possesses his ultimate good by way of his own knowledge. The seventh Beatitude describes this possession of God more in terms of a common possession. Peace is a common good enjoyed among many persons, and membership in a family, to be a child of God, also implies a kind of common possession. Just as many children can have one father in common, so too the peacemakers can have God as a common possession with his other children.

So when we consider this eighth Beatitude, we can understand what is implied in the reward "the kingdom of heaven." A kingdom also implies common membership, but in an even more expansive way than a family does. A kingdom is composed of many families. And so to contemplate God, to possess him by way of loving knowledge as a member of a kingdom, is to share him in an even more expansive way than to share him as a member of the same family. And just as the common good of the family is greater than the private good of an individual member of that family, so also the common good of the kingdom is an even greater common good than that of the family. In some way, then, this reward seems to be emphasizing the goodness of the reward of possessing God precisely as a common good.

It is better, for example, that God be the God not only of Abraham or Isaac or Jacob but of the whole Jewish people.[66] And it is better for God to be the God not only of the Jewish people but also of the Gentiles. And this universality, this catholicity, of possessing God is itself a cause of tremendous joy. For we will love our neighbor as ourselves, and so our joy will grow in proportion to the number of those who possess God. St. Thomas teaches this very fact:

> For each one will love his neighbor as himself, and, therefore, he will rejoice in the good of his neighbor as in his own

good. As a result, the joy of each one will be increased to the degree that the joy of all increases. As is said in Psalm 86 (v.7), "The dwelling in thee is as it were of all rejoicing."[67]

In his letter to the Hebrews, St. Paul describes the joys of possessing God as members of a kingdom very beautifully:

You have come to Mount Zion and to the city of the living God, the heavenly Jerusalem, and to innumerable angels in festal gathering, and to the assembly of the first-born who are enrolled in heaven, and to a judge who is God of all, and to the spirits of just men made perfect" (Heb. 12:22–23).

So there is a special joy, a particular beatitude, associated with this possession of God as a member of the heavenly kingdom.

There is another aspect to the reward implied by "the kingdom of heaven." Not only will those persecuted for the sake of righteousness be admitted to membership in the kingdom of heaven, but they shall also *reign* in this kingdom, sharing the power and glory of Christ their king. Thus Jesus says, "You are those who have continued with me in my trials; as my Father appointed a kingdom for me, so do I appoint for you, that you may eat and drink at my table in my kingdom, and sit on thrones judging the twelve tribes of Israel" (Luke 22:28–30).

It is also clear why this reward is appropriate to those who have been persecuted for the sake of righteousness. For it is fitting and just that those who have been driven out of an earthly kingdom for the sake of God should be admitted to his heavenly kingdom. This is how Paul describes the faith of the holy patriarchs and prophets:

By faith Abraham obeyed when he was called to go out to a place which he was to receive as an inheritance; and he went out, not knowing where he was to go. By faith he sojourned in the land of promise, as in a foreign land, living in tents with Isaac and Jacob, heirs with him of the same promise. For he looked forward to the city which has foundations, whose builder and maker is God (Heb. 11:8–10).

He then concludes by recounting the persecution they suffered for the sake of membership in that heavenly city:

Some were tortured, refusing to accept release, that they might rise again to a better life. Others suffered mocking and scourging, and even chains and imprisonment. They were stoned, they were sawn in two, they were killed with the sword; they went about in skins of sheep and goats, destitute, afflicted, ill-treated—of whom the world was not worthy—wandering over deserts and mountains, and in dens and caves of the earth. And all these, though well attested by their faith, did not receive what was promised, since God had foreseen something better for us, that apart from us they should not be made perfect (Heb. 11:35–40).

It is also just that those who have been judged unjustly should be established as just judges over others. Therefore, it is appropriate that those who have been persecuted for the sake of justice should be made judges over others: "the saints will judge the world" (1 Cor. 6:2).

Overcoming difficulties in living out this Beatitude

This Beatitude is truly the most difficult to live. And many Christians think that living this Beatitude is optional. Yet it is the unambiguous teaching of Jesus and his apostles that all who are true disciples of Jesus will suffer persecution: "Remember the word that I said to you, 'A servant is not greater than his master.' If they persecuted me, they will persecute you" (John 15:20). And Paul reiterates: "Indeed all who desire to live a godly life in Christ Jesus will be persecuted" (2 Tim. 3:12). On one occasion, considering whether many or only a few people would have the opportunity for martyrdom, St. Thomas Aquinas said that if a man speaks the truth his entire life as he ought, he will almost certainly find himself in danger of death. So persecution is inescapable for the true follower of Jesus. That is the first step in living out this Beatitude: we must accept that it will be our lot.

Another consideration that helps us to live out this Beatitude is to recognize that whether we suffer for Christ or not, we shall still suffer. All of us will die, and there is no such thing as a comfortable or easy death. I do not know whether dying of cancer is any easier than dying by persecution. We will lose our life: why not lose it for the sake of Jesus Christ that he might preserve it for us in eternal life? He is no fool who gives up what he cannot keep for the sake of what he cannot lose.

Ultimately, however, it is hope for eternal life and the gifts of the Holy Spirit that allow us to practice and experience this Beatitude. Those who are moved by the gifts of the Holy Spirit do not avoid persecution, nor do they simply endure persecution. Instead, they seek it out and rejoice in it!

Paul eloquently exhorts his fellow Christians to embrace this last Beatitude:

Since we are surrounded by so great a cloud of witnesses, let us also lay aside every weight, and sin which clings so closely, and let us run with perseverance the race that is set before us, looking to Jesus the pioneer and perfecter of our faith, who for the joy that was set before him endured the cross, despising the shame, and is seated at the right hand of the throne of God. Consider him who endured from sinners such hostility against himself, so that you may not grow weary or fainthearted. In your struggle against sin you have not yet resisted to the point of shedding your blood. And have you forgotten the exhortation which addresses you as sons? "My son, do not regard lightly the discipline of the Lord, nor lose courage when you are punished by him. For the Lord disciplines him whom he loves, and chastises every son whom he receives" (Heb. 12:1–6).

It is for the sake of the joy that lies before us that we are enabled to practice this Beatitude. To the degree that hope is strong, to that same degree joy is made present. And when that hope-caused joy is great, it allows us to overcome the bodily sorrows of the present moment.

When all is said and done, none of us has the strength to endure great persecution. So what is needed most of all is trust that our loving Father will come to our aid in our time of need. It was said about St. Lawrence that as he lay upon the grill, it seemed as if one person was suffering and another was speaking. And St. Perpetua did not even notice the violence done to her body by the wild beasts. It was Christ who suffered in them, it was Christ who conquered in them:

And when they bring you to trial and deliver you up, do not be anxious beforehand what you are to say; but say whatever is given you in that hour, for it is not you who speak, but the Holy Spirit. And brother will deliver up brother to death, and the father his child, and children will rise against parents and have them put to death; and you will be hated by all for my name's sake. But he who endures to the end will be saved (Mark 13:11–13).

More than any other Beatitude, living out this Beatitude means allowing Christ to live within us, to suffer within us, to die within us: "I have been crucified with Christ. It is no longer I who live, but Christ who lives in me; and the life I now live in the flesh I live by faith in the Son of God, who loved me and gave himself for me" (Gal. 2:20).

The example of Christ and the saints

Jesus suffered persecution throughout his public life, but especially at the end. He taught that our righteousness must exceed the righteousness of the scribes and the Pharisees, for which reason they persecuted him. He taught that all, even the Pharisees, had need of repentance and the mercy of God. For which they persecuted him even more. Finally, he was scourged, crowned with thorns, and crucified because he refused to deny that he was God. In all these things, Christ left us an example of suffering for the sake of truth and righteousness.

For one is approved if, mindful of God, he endures pain while suffering unjustly. For what credit is it, if when you do wrong and are beaten for it you take it patiently? But if when you do right and suffer for it you take it patiently, you have God's approval. For to this you have been called, because Christ also suffered for you, leaving you an example, that you should follow in his steps (1 Pet. 2:19–21).

Many, many saints were extraordinary examples of joyfully suffering persecution for the sake of righteousness. We have, for example, the beautiful testimony of St. Ambrose that clearly manifests how St. Sebastian lived out this final Beatitude. Ambrose writes:

> To enter the kingdom of God we must endure many tribulations. If there are many persecutions, there are many testings; where there are many crowns of victory, there are many trials of strength. It is then to your advantage if there are many persecutors; among many persecutions, you may more easily find a path to victory. Take the example of the martyr Sebastian, whose birthday in glory we celebrate today. He was a native of Milan. At a time when persecution either had ceased or had not yet begun or was of a milder kind, he realized that there was only slight, if any, opportunity for suffering. He set out for Rome, where bitter persecutions were raging because of the fervor of the Christians. There he endured suffering; there he gained his crown. He went to the city as a stranger and there established a home of undying glory. If there had been only one persecutor, he would not have gained a martyr's crown.[68]

Notice that Sebastian came to Rome not only to assist the suffering Christians but also to have the opportunity to live this last Beatitude. And what is more striking still: after he was pierced with arrows and left to die, he recovered and offered his life again for Christ. It is one thing if someone, ignorant of the suffering he is about to endure, exposes his life to danger. It is another to do so after having experienced firsthand what that suffering is like!

Sebastian, following Jesus, taught us that the natural habitat of the Christian in this world is persecution. His faith reflected the faith of the early Church in the age of martyrs: an age in which Christians were enthusiastic about the opportunity to offer their life for Jesus Christ and to secure for themselves eternal life on high with him. This final Beatitude condemns the lukewarmness of our modern times and inspires us to joyfully look forward to times of persecution with confidence that it is Christ who will fight with us and in us to save us.

The last Beatitude and the gift of final perseverance

Our Lord links this final Beatitude to the gift of final perseverance. In the Gospel of Mark he says, "Brother will hand over brother to death, and the father his child; children will rise up against parents and have them put to death. You will be hated by all because of my name. But the one who perseveres to the end will be saved" (13:12–13, NAB). And in Matthew he says something similar:

> Then they will deliver you up to tribulation, and put you to death; and you will be hated by all nations for my name's sake. And then many will fall away, and betray one another, and hate one another. And many false prophets will arise and lead many astray. And because wickedness is multiplied, most men's love will grow cold. But he who endures to the end will be saved (24:9–13).

This instruction of Jesus manifests why this eighth Beatitude comes last among the Beatitudes. Just as the grace of final perseverance is the completion of the grace of conversion and the crown of a life lived for Jesus Christ, so is the eighth Beatitude the completion and crown of the previous Beatitudes. We tend to think of persecution as a punishment or a sign of God's disfavor. In reality, it is culmination of a life lived for Christ and like Christ. Persecution is a sign of predestination and the gift of final perseverance.

DO NOT BE AFRAID OF HAPPINESS!

We are now at the end of this series of meditations upon the Beatitudes, the heart of Christ's gospel. Somewhere along the way, my dear reader, I hope that you have become convinced that the Beatitudes are not just a list from eighth-grade catechism class, but a program for your entire life, God's plan for working out your happiness. That is already an important step. But it is not enough. Now comes the challenge of beginning to live the Beatitudes and persevering in that life.

For most people, the obstacle they face in seriously living out this teaching of Jesus is *fear*. It is a fear much like that of a skydiver about to jump out of his first airplane. It is the fear of not wanting to let go of control over your own life and your own plans about how to make yourself happy. How can I be sure that Jesus loves me more than I love myself? How can I trust that he will really take care of me if I go all-in on his teaching?

Most people's spiritual lives are actually a constant attempt to simultaneously fulfill the bare minimum of the commandments while maintaining the maximum amount of control over their own lives. They have one foot on the shore and the other in the water . . . while Jesus calls them to go out with him into the deep. The Beatitudes are a condemnation of that attitude. They shout, "Let go! Trust in God with all your heart!"

The beautiful thing is that living the Beatitudes is indeed much like skydiving. Once you've done it, the hesitation and apprehension almost entirely disappears, and you are left only with the exhilarating experience of allowing yourself to free-fall, confident that you will make it safely to your destination. So it is with the Beatitudes: you only need to let go once, and you become convinced that Jesus will take care of you going forward.

As a vowed religious, I had to make that leap at the moment of my solemn profession, when I promised poverty, chastity, and obedience for the remainder of my life. It was frightening, yet Jesus has more than fulfilled his promise to take care of me and make me happier than I ever could have done on my own. So don't be afraid.

The next step after taking the leap to live the Beatitudes is to become a witness of Jesus' loving providence and care to others. After delivering these eight Beatitudes to the people, the next words of Jesus are an incitement to evangelization: "You are the salt of the earth . . . You are the light of the world" (Matt. 5:13–14). Happiness is too good to keep to yourself. It is more possible for the sun not to shine and give warmth than for the Christian not to evangelize with words and deeds.

Remember: the greatest goods are those able to be shared by many without diminishing. So beatitude, more than any other good, is able to be shared. God wills to share his blessed happiness with us, and he wants us to become instruments of bringing it to others, so that we might all rejoice as his children in his kingdom of eternal joy.

Fr. Sebastian Walshe is a Norbertine canon of the Abbey of St. Michael in the Diocese of Orange, California. After earning a degree in electrical engineering, Fr. Sebastian worked at an intellectual property firm before pursuing further education at Thomas Aquinas College. Graduating in 1994, he continued studies at the Catholic University of America in Washington D.C., receiving a license in philosophy. Later, while in the seminary, he attended the Pontifical University of St. Thomas at Rome (the Angelicum) where he received a master's degree in sacred theology and a doctorate in philosophy. Since 2006, Fr. Sebastian has been a professor of philosophy in the seminary program at St. Michael's Abbey, where he is the dean of studies.

ENDNOTES

1   This analogy governing the Scriptures was well known to the Fathers of the Church and recently reasserted in *Dei Verbum*: "The words of God, expressed in human language, have been made like human discourse, just as the Word of the eternal Father, when he took to himself the flesh of human weakness, was in every way made like men" (13; cf. CCC 101).

2   Some ancient texts, such as the Latin Vulgate edition, have this Beatitude switched with the previous Beatitude ("Blessed are those who mourn").

3   See also Romans 2:6–8: "God will repay everyone according to his works: eternal life to those who seek glory, honor, and immortality through perseverance in good works."

4   However, Matthew does record a list of woes addressed to the Pharisees and scribes in the twenty-third chapter of his Gospel, which in some way can be seen to correspond as contraries to the Beatitudes.

5   *Summa Theologiae*, I–II, q.69, a.3, resp.6.

6   St. Thomas: "All these rewards are one in reality, namely eternal happiness, which the human understanding cannot grasp. And, therefore, it was necessary that they be described through different goods which are known to us." (*Summa Theologiae*, I–II, q.69, a.4, resp.1).

7   See St. Thomas's commentary on the *Sentences* of Peter Lombard: "It ought to be known that this plurality of notions about God comes about from the fact that what God is exceeds our intellect. For our intellect is not able to receive diverse modes of perfections under one conception: both since it receives its knowledge from creatures, in which there are diverse modes of perfections according to their diverse forms, and also since that which is one and simple in God, would be diversified in our intellect even if we were to receive it immediately from God, just as the procession of his goodness in other creatures is multiplied. Whence, since God, according to one and the same thing, is perfect in every way, one conception is not able to apprehend his perfection integrally, and consequently, neither are we able to name his

perfection with one name. And therefore it is necessary that the intellect
have different conceptions of him," (*In I Sent.*, D.2, q.1, a.3).

8   *Summa Theologiae*, I–II, q.69, a.3, resp.4.

9   Letter to Proba, Ep. 130, 13.

10   *Summa Theologiae*, I–II, q.69, a.2, resp.3

11   *Diary of St. Faustina*, 770–771.

12   *Super Ev. Matt*, lect.2. It is obvious that the first three opinions are rejected
by the Lord, but it is not as clear that he rejects the opinion that happiness
consists in the contemplation of God, since one of the Beatitudes is
"blessed are the pure of heart, for they will see God." St. Thomas explains
by saying "The Lord rejects the opinion of those who say that beatitude
consists in the contemplation of divine things with regard to the time in
which it takes place [i.e., the present life] . . . hence he says they *will* see.

13   *Summa Theologiae*, I–II, q.66, a.2, c.

14   Homily on the Beatitudes.

15   Students of moral philosophy will notice that those who mourn and the
meek correspond to the two powers of the sense appetite: the concupiscible
and irascible appetites.

16   St. Thomas Aquinas teaches that there are two kinds of common good: a
common good that is intrinsic to the community who share in it (such as
peace or justice in a society, which is a kind of order within the society
itself) and a common good that is extrinsic to the community who share
in it (such as a child is a common good of both his parents). Of the two,
the extrinsic common good is better than the intrinsic common good.
An example of this is in an army, which the intrinsic order of the army is
for the sake of fulfilling the will of the general to obtain victory. An even
clearer example is in the order of the universe, which is for the sake of
fulfilling the will of God. The intrinsic common good is for the sake of the
extrinsic common good, so that the extrinsic common good is better and
more noble.

17   Human beings are perfected not only by goods pertaining to their
individual nature, but also by goods pertaining to their natural
membership in a family and their natural membership in civil society. And
the more perfect the society to which they belong, the more perfect are the
goods. A human being is brought to greater perfection within civil society
than if he had been raised in a good family apart from any civil society (for

example, someone raised in civil society has an opportunity for a better education). So also, the rewards promised in the Beatitudes mirror this ascending order of goods.

18 *Mystery and Manners: Occasional Prose*, 34.

19 I want to acknowledge and thank Dr. Michael Augros for suggesting many of these questions, as well as for his own thoughts he has shared with me concerning the Beatitudes over the years. Some of those thoughts influenced my own ideas and are reflected in my treatment of the Beatitudes contained below.

20 Something similar happens when a penitent comes to confession. The very fact that he is there is positive evidence to the priest that he is sorry for his sins.

21 Leo the Great, Sermon on the Beatitudes.

22 *Summa Contra Gentiles* III, c.135.

23 See *Summa Theologiae*, I–II, q.69, a.1.

24 *Compendium of Theology*, Part II, chapter 2.

25 Homily on the Sermon on the Mount.

26 Ibid.

27 *Summa Theologiae*, II–II, q.83, a.9, resp.3.

28 Some sensible goods are easy to obtain whereas others are difficult to obtain. From this distinction, there arise two powers of the sense appetite: the *concupiscible* appetite, which is the power ordained to pursuing and enjoying readily available goods (think of someone enjoying a bowl of ice cream), and the *irascible* appetite, which is the power ordained to pursuing and obtaining goods which are difficult to get (think of someone traveling a long distance to visit his girlfriend).

29 *Disputed Questions on Truth*, Q.26, a.10, ad.10.

30 Sermon on the Beatitudes.

31 Sermon on the Beatitudes.

32 *The Passion and Death of Jesus Christ.*

33 See *Summa Theologiae*, III, q.46, a.8.

34 See *Summa Theologiae*, III, q.46, a.6 and *In III Sent.*, d.15, q.2, a.3c.

35 Sermon on the Sunday in the Octave of the Assumption, from the Office of Readings on the feast of Our Lady of Sorrows, September 15.

36 Letter to Doctor Castillo, from the Office of Readings for her feast day, August 23.

37 *Summa Theologiae*, I–II, q.69, a.3. Also see I–II, q.35, a.3, resp.1: "The sorrows of the present life lead us to the comfort of the future life. Because by the mere fact that man mourns for his sins, or for the delay of glory, he merits the consolation of eternity. In like manner a man merits it when he shrinks not from hardships and straits in order to obtain it."

38 Also, see Mark 3:5, which describes Jesus as being angry.

39 Sermon on the Beatitudes.

40 Commentary on the Our Father, a.2.

41 Homily on the Sermon on the Mount.

42 From *Mother Teresa's Secret Fire* by Joseph Langford, 281–2.

43 Prayer for Justice, St. Teresa of Calcutta.

44 Sermon on the Beatitudes.

45 *Summa Theologiae*, I–II, q.69, a.4, c.

46 See *Summa Theologiae*, II–II, q.32, a.2.

47 *Diary of St. Faustina*, n.163.

48 Commentary on the Lord's Prayer, a.5.

49 *Confessions*, Book X.

50 *De Diabolo Tentatore*, 2.

51 *Summa Theologiae*, I, q.2, a.3, obj.1.

52 In spite of the inscription on that photograph, there is some dispute about whether the photograph actually took place at the canonization. Nevertheless, it is certain that the mother of St. Maria forgave Alessandro, and that the photograph depicts them sitting peacefully together.

53 Sermon on the Beatitudes.

54 This is often expressed by the Latin phrase *ex opere operato*, which means "from the work having been done."

55 *Diary of St. Faustina*, n.770–771.

56 *Summa Theologiae*, II–II, q.83, a.9, resp.3.

57 *Summa Theologiae*, I–II, q.69, a.3, resp.

58 Why are they called "sons" of God rather than "children" of God? Does this somehow exclude women? The use of the expression "sons" is not meant to exclude women but rather to highlight the likeness of peacemakers to Jesus who is the natural Son of God, as well as to the angels, who are referred to in Scripture as "sons" of God. So this should not be taken as referring exclusively to the male sex.

59 *Summa Theologiae*, I–II, q.69, a.4, c.

60 See the Rule of St. Augustine.

61 Sermon on the Beatitudes.

62 To take a simple example, the order among notes on a guitar is founded upon a more fundamental order among numbers. Higher notes are produced by a greater number of vibrations of the guitar strings.

63 *Vita Norberti* B, I,I 7.

64 *On the Lord's Prayer*, a.7.

65 *Summa Theologiae*, I–II, q.69, a.3, resp. 5.

66 St. Paul asserts this in striking terms when he says: "For I could wish that I myself were accursed and cut off from Christ for the sake of my brethren, my kinsmen by race" (Rom. 9:3).

67 *Commentary on the Apostle's Creed*, a.12.

68 Taken from the Office of Readings on the feast of St. Sebastian.